# Break a Leg!

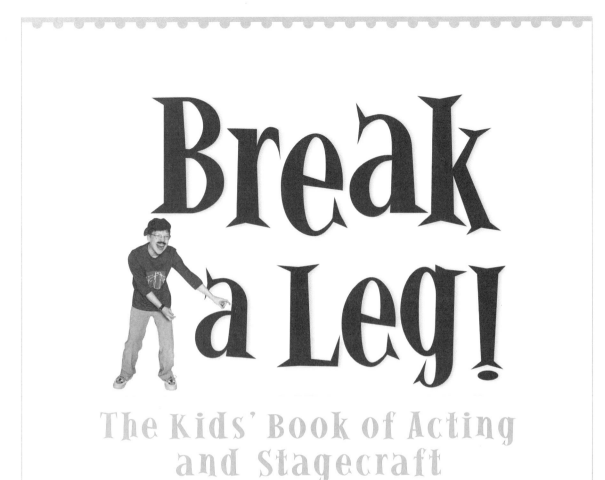

# Break a Leg!

## The Kids' Book of Acting and Stagecraft

### Lise Friedman

#### Photographs by Mary Dowdle

WORKMAN PUBLISHING • NEW YORK

To Tony,
for his love, patience,
and unflagging sense of humor.

Text copyright © 2002 Lise Friedman
Photographs copyright © 2002 Mary Dowdle
(For other art credits, please see page 222.)

Library of Congress Cataloging-in-Publication Data
Friedman, Lise.
Break a leg! : the kids' guide to acting and stagecraft / by Lise Friedman.
p. cm.
Summary: A comprehensive manual for acting and theater, discussing
improvisation, voice projection, breathing exercises, script analysis, and
technical aspects of theater production.

ISBN 0-7611-2208-7 (alk. paper)—ISBN 0-7611-2590-6
1. Acting–Juvenile literature. [1. Acting. 2. Theater—Production and direction.]
I. Title.
PN2061 .F75 2001
792'.028—dc21                                          2001026986

Workman Publishing Company, Inc.
708 Broadway
New York, NY 10003-9555
www.workman.com

Manufactured in the United States of America
First printing February 2002
10 9 8 7 6 5 4 3 2 1

# Acknowledgments

*B*reak a Leg! came into being through the efforts and largesse of many talented people. Bravos all around.

Stephanie Berlic, Marcus Cave, Valeria Congliani, Joey di Conzetto, Melanie Dionisio, Evynne Duckman, Patrick Duffey, Rashad Farmer, Jennifer Grant, Molly Haylor, Sophie Mascatello, Max Shultz-Reid, and David Tay are the kids who posed and were so forthcoming with their perceptions.

Michelle Audet of City Lights Youth Theatre, Peter Jensen of the American Academy of Dramatic Arts, Peggy Lewis of Biz Kids, Arthur Penn and the Actors Studio, Katie Watts of The Lee Strasberg Theatre Institute, and Jean Taylor of Lincoln Center Institute opened the doors to their schools, students, and methods.

Photographer Mary Dowdle captured moment after magic moment. Stylist Karla Martinez, makeup artist Noelle Marinelli, and Ruth Garcia infused the project with a sense of theater and fun. The generosity of James Galloway of Studio with a View, Paul Dempsy of SoHo Studios, Laura Lang of Calumet Photography, and Barbara Hitchcock of Polaroid Corporation ensured we had space, equipment, and film.

Lighting designer Benjamin Pearcy, set and costume designer Venustiano Borromeo, sound designer Michael Creason, and photographer

*A big hug to all of our friends from Charlie Chaplin and Hank Mann from the film* City Lights *(1931).*

Michal Daniel generously granted the use of their designs and images. Actor Marlene Forte, film director Ruth Sergel, theater director Steven Maler, professor Katherine Maus, dance teacher and choreographer Ellen Robbins, Judith Stiles and actor Julia Stiles, stage manager Colman Rupp, prop designer Zeke Leonard, sound designer Andy Bryant, film enthusiast Dean Swanson, stage combat expert Ricki Ravitts, Carla Steen of the Guthrie Theater, and Carol Fineman, Vincent de Marco, and Jordan Shapiro of the Joseph Papp Public Theater/New York Shakespeare Festival provided invaluable input and access.

Thanks to the staff of Workman Publishing: to art director Paul Gamarello and designers Janet Vicario and Natsumi Uda, who brought the book to life on the page; to the tireless and first-class expediter Cindy Schoen; and above all, to my editor, Liz Carey, for her sharp insights and enthusiasm.

To my agent, Wendy Sherman, special thanks.

# Contents

# Foreword
## by Julia Stiles

When I started acting professionally, I had absolutely no idea what I was doing. I had nothing to help me navigate in the acting world, and so I relied largely on trial and error. As an only child living in our large New York City loft, I entertained myself by playing dress-up and mimicking performances I had seen on television. In essence, I was my own imaginary friend. I knew nothing about auditioning, technique, or memorizing lines. All I knew was that I loved imitating what I carefully observed in other people, and the thrill of performing. Everything I did to launch a career as an actress happened on a whim.

Being the daring, but naïve, pre-adolescent I was, I wrote a letter to a bizarre experimental theater company, hoping to be given a spot in one of their shows. The founders of Ridge Theater gave me a test run, a three-line part in its fall production, entitled *Jungle Movie.* I had enough chutzpah to figure that my instinct would make up for the experience I lacked. Our first night of rehearsals I remember the director

Jungle Movie, *Ridge Theater (1992)*

announcing to the adult company, "Take five, everybody!" I excused my eleven-year-old self, called my father, and whispered into the phone, "Dad, what does 'take five' mean? Is it time to go home?"

Since then I have learned that "take five" is a signal for a five-minute break, and I've added numerous other tidbits to my acting vocabulary. I've never gone to drama school, but I have my own scrapbook of information that I have collected in the nine years I've been a working actor. I record everything from random epiphanies I've had on movie sets to quotes I gather just from watching *Inside the Actors Studio.* I've gathered my own bible of acting, partly because I love the process of exploring this rewarding craft, and partly because I have always felt the need for some sort of guide.

This book is its own sort of bible of acting. It contains just about everything you need to know about acting as a profession. The information collected here is easy to read, fun, and creative. You certainly need not take the entire book as gospel, but you will probably find most of it handy. I only wish it had been published nine years ago so I could have read it then! The most important thing to remember is that there is no right or wrong in playing pretend. You, as an individual, are like a musical instrument ready to strike chords in the human spirit. This book can help you with any fine-tuning you might need.

# Introduction

## All the World's a Stage

William Shakespeare wasn't exaggerating when he wrote those famous words. Performances of all kinds are going on just about everywhere you look and listen: at the movies, in auditoriums, on television, on the radio, in school gymnasiums, community centers, theaters, and camps—even in the streets and on the World Wide Web. Sometimes it seems as if the acting bug has bitten the entire planet.

What's all of this acting about, anyway? What is the matter with real life? Nothing at all. In fact, theater not only takes you on flights of fantasy; it

*William Shakespeare, circa 1600*

**drama:** the performance of an imaginary or real-life situation that involves a plot, theme, characters, some sort of conflict, and usually some sort of resolution

makes you look with brand-new eyes at the **drama** of the everyday world, and at how the conflicts and resolutions that happen in your own life can help you create and maintain the illusion of reality on the stage or screen.

Maybe you've already "trod the boards"—that's slang for acting—and are thinking about your next step. Or maybe you have never set foot on a stage or stood in front of a camera and are simply curious about what you might find there. Either way, now that you've cracked the cover of *Break a Leg!*, you'll not only get an overview of what it means to be an actor;

you will learn all about what it takes to get there and how to do it.

You'll find loads of interactive info about the **craft** itself, including how to improvise and develop a scene, create a character, fake a slap across the face, prepare for an audition, manage stage fright, and get on- and offstage without tumbling into the pit.

**craft:** the various artistic techniques that enable an actor to express him- or herself

You'll discover that your body and the voice that comes out of it are your major acting instruments. Like all instruments of expression, they need to be cared for and fine-tuned. You already know a lot about how they work—you've been using them both for your entire life, after all. But do you know how your posture, gestures, even the way you walk and talk speak volumes about who you are? There's an old saying that the body never lies. As an actor, you don't tune into and out of life. You live it and breathe it, twenty-four hours a day, seven days a week. You're always observing others and discovering new ways to interpret what you see and feel. These observations are like money in the bank, soaking up interest until you're ready to put them to work.

Next time you're out and about, pay close attention to the people around you. A person's body language and tone of voice tell you all sorts of things about his or her attitude, mood, confidence, and frame of mind. All of these observations help you get at the essence of behavior. For example, if you pay close attention you'll notice that people don't have just one emotion at a time. You can simultaneously be really mad at your mother and still feel strong love for her. If you can show both of those emotions through your acting, it's much closer to real life, and ultimately much more powerful for the audience. There are many exercises specially designed to help you sharpen your powers of observation and interpretation.

In addition to learning about the craft of acting, this book will give you the inside scoop on rehearsal and performance manners. How you behave toward the director, your fellow actors, and the crew really does matter. Your reputation can precede you like a stink bomb or a breath of fresh air.

And you will find intriguing bits of history, lingo, and amazing legends, tips about the complex business of being an actor, and an overview of the behind-the-scenes action that makes it all happen without a hitch. Bet you didn't know that there are intricate plots behind the sound and lighting designs.

**mediums:** the different types of media where you might find acting, including TV, the radio, theater, and the Web

Since you're never off acting duty, you'll want to choose one thing to do every day to improve your craft. Go to a movie, watch commercials, tune in to a serious TV drama or a comedy, listen to the radio, go to see a play. Get to know the different **mediums.** Did you know that every single commercial and every cartoon voice-over is a job for an actor? What do you see yourself doing? Get involved and take chances. Try different classes. Audition for school and community productions. Help build a set. Read plays. Write your own! There's a universe of possibilities. The more you explore, the more you'll learn about the great big world of acting and, most important, about yourself.

No matter what you end up doing when you grow up, the skills and sensitivities that you acquire through acting can and will help you go farther wherever your interests and talents may lead you. You'll have the poise that comes with an awareness and a command of your body and voice, you'll be comfortable speaking in public, you'll be more conscious of other people's feelings—and you'll have a great memory, thanks to learning all of those lines.

# Take the Plunge

Before you get into the all-important body and voice exercises that every actor learns in acting class, take the plunge and try a *monologue,* which is a speech for a single actor. Though we don't usually go around reciting speeches for anyone who will listen, monologues are a handy dramatic device that playwrights and screenwriters use to reveal a character's interior life, a kind of thinking and feeling out loud. Monologues can also be used to comment on offstage or background action. And when performed in auditions, they are a great way for a director to see an actor's particular acting skills and qualities. If you've ever spoken in front of your class, you already have a sense of what's involved.

> **David** *Monologues can be very interesting. When you do one, try not to sound monotonic. Keep your facial expressions and the tone of your voice alive. Don't use too many physical motions, like flapping your arms.*

Choose one of the monologues for a boy or girl in the Appendix at the back of the book, and read through it a few times. Try to get a sense of the character's age, mood, body language, and how he or she might sound. When you're ready, give it a whirl. Don't worry about memorizing the lines. That part comes later.

> **Jen** *I just have to say that monologues are difficult. They're one of the more annoying things until you know how to do them. I love to do them when I'm prepared because they allow you to be in control of the audition situation.*

How did you do? If you felt awkward, that's perfectly okay. It's not easy to slip into someone else's shoes. You will try again—and be amazed at the differences—after you've done some body, voice, and character work.

# Meet the Cast!

**R**eady to get started? Then say hello to the cast of *Break a Leg!* Joey and Patrick are twelve- and thirteen-year-old actors who have appeared in radio and TV commercials and had a taste of the Great White Way (that's show-biz slang for Broadway). Eleven-year-old Evynne has sung in a show at Madison Square Garden. David, thirteen, has worked in two Broadway shows and starred in the award-winning movie *A Cup of Coffee.* Eighteen-year-old Jen (not pictured) co-wrote and performed in Off-off-Broadway's *Knee-high to a Microphone,* a play for and about teens. Sophie, fourteen, acted in the independent movie *Cusp.* And ten-year-olds Rashad and Melanie, eleven-year-olds Valeria and Stephanie, and twelve-year-olds Marcus, Max, and Molly are just beginning their performing careers. All are eager to share their experiences and offer perspectives and pearls of wisdom as they demonstrate exercises and fill you in on everything from coping with rejection and learning lines to performing for the camera, tackling Shakespeare, and crying on cue!

Melanie

Marcus

Max

Joey

Sophie

David

Rashad

Molly

Stephanie

Patrick

Evynne

Valeria

# chapter one

# Body Basics

*Tuning Your Instrument • Body Warm-ups • Stretches*

All actors, even the most famous, know that the more they do to increase their physical fitness, sensitivity, and awareness, the more in tune and responsive to acting their bodies will be. If you participate in sports, dance, yoga, martial arts, or gymnastics, great. Don't stop! Your body is a flexible instrument that improves with use. If you are a couch potato, try to find an activity that gets you moving. You'll not only look and feel better, you'll banish bad habits like slouching to one side, hiking up your shoulders, or jiggling your knees, which cause tension and tightening and can inhibit your all-important emotional expression.

★ **Patrick** *You need to stretch out your whole body so you don't pull anything when you start to move.*

The following exercises are typical of what you will find in any number of acting classes. Each is designed to warm up and stretch different parts of your body, so it's helpful if you do them before you begin rehearsing or working on a character. It's best to exercise where you have room to lie down and extend your arms and legs. Be sure to wear comfortable clothing that allows you to move freely. Sweatpants or leggings and a T-shirt and bare feet or socks are just fine. Try to work calmly and carefully, without strain. Never force your body into an uncomfortable position. The idea is to prepare your body for acting, not the Olympics! When you become accustomed to the exercises, feel free to do them to music, change the order, even make up your own.

**Stacking Blocks** This is a great way to wake up your body. Standing with your feet comfortably apart, stretch your arms way above your head, keeping your neck long and shoulders relaxed. As you stretch, inhale deeply. Then, starting with your hands, wrists, and elbows, release your stretch, allowing your arms, head, and torso to curl forward as you gently bend your knees and release your breath. Stay in that curled position for a moment and breathe in and out slowly. Now roll up carefully through your spine until you are in the original upright position. Repeat a few times, stretching, releasing, curling, and breathing a bit more fully each time.

★ **Stephanie** *Warm-up exercises help me go to new limits. When I stretch I feel more relaxed and like I can do more with my acting.*

★ **Joey** *Warm-up exercises are really important to train your body. Always remember to stretch.*

**Get the Kinks Out** Give your torso a good stretch. Standing upright, swing your arms from side to side across your body. Once you get a smooth, swooping action going, swing your arms forward and backward and in a big spiral around your torso. Keep breathing. Allow your waist and hips to twist and your knees to bend as you swing. Notice the arc your arms make as they swing down and up again, and feel how the weight of your hands seems to change as you play with the size and speed of your swings.

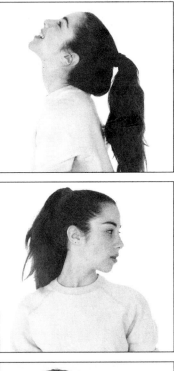

**Heavy Head** Use the weight of your head to lengthen your neck and relax your shoulders. Standing in a relaxed upright position with your arms at your sides, let your head gently drop forward toward your chest. Don't bounce. Now slowly lift your head and look up at the ceiling—or sky, if you're lucky enough to be exercising outdoors. Allow your mouth to open slightly to relax your jaw. Slowly come back to center. Close your mouth! Turn your head to your right, keeping your shoulders facing forward. Now left. Face forward and let your right ear drop toward your shoulder. Feel a

stretch along the left side of your neck. Lift to center and drop toward the other shoulder. Now make a half circle, dropping your head to one shoulder and circling it first forward, then to the other side. Then reverse. Allow the weight of your head to determine the stretch. Come back to center and lift your shoulders toward your ears. You're a turtle trying to disappear into your shell. Hold this scrunched position for a moment—don't forget to breathe—then release. Ahhhh. Repeat a few times, then lift and drop one shoulder at a time, followed by shoulder circles forward and back. Your neck should feel five miles long.

**Get Hippy** Give your waist and hips a good stretch. Standing with your legs slightly apart, place your hands on your hips and face forward. Tilt to your right side, bending at your waist. Allow your head to drop toward the floor. Return to center and tilt to your left. Come back to center and bend forward, keeping your back as straight as possible and your neck long. Take a good look at the floor. Now come upright again and lean back from your waist, keeping your head facing forward. Repeat a few times.

**Tightrope Walker** How's your balance? Starting from an upright position with your weight evenly on both feet, shift to your left side and bend your right knee slightly as you lift your right foot a few inches off the floor. You may want to use your arms to help you balance. Now swing your right leg back and forward a few times, brushing your toes against the floor. Reach higher with each swing. Not too high; you don't want to topple over. Repeat on the other side.

**Meow** This spine stretch is a bit complicated, so take your time. Sit on your heels and bend forward over your knees, reaching your arms along the floor in front of you. Now, take a nice deep breath and exhale as you slide your head and torso forward along the floor, stretching your spine long. Inhale gently as you slowly press your weight onto your palms, straighten your arms, and raise your chest. Keeping your motion as catlike as possible, round your spine toward the ceiling and let your head drop forward. Exhale. As you return to your original sitting position, inhale slowly. Repeat.

**Stretch and Melt** Sit up straight and make a diamond with your legs and feet: heels together, knees reaching toward the floor. Gently hold your ankles as you lower your torso and head forward. You want to feel the stretch along your spine and the insides of your legs. Breathe. Roll up gently and repeat. Now open your legs in a wide **V** and reach overhead with your arms. Try to keep your spine and legs long. Now stretch your arms over your right leg, reaching for your ankle. Hold the position a moment; try to touch your forehead to your knee. Breathe. Return to center and stretch to your left. Now lie down, rolling carefully through your spine, and relax. Concentrate on your breathing as you feel your weight sink into the floor. Don't fall asleep! When you're ready, roll slowly onto one side and stand up.

**Look Before You Leap** Time to look around. Really look. Be conscious of your breath as you take in the colors and shapes of the room. Now stretch your spine long and bounce your knees gently, feeling the spring in your ankles and feet. Take the bounce from side to side, forward and back, allowing your hips, torso, head, and arms to react. Make your movements larger and larger as you bounce around the room. Don't be surprised if you feel the urge to sing. Gradually, slow down and return to a still position.

**Time to Dance** Now you get to pull it all together! Pick a color, any color, and a body part, any part. Let's say you choose yellow and your right ear. Yes, it seems silly, but hang in there! Take a few moments to explore the qualities of your color through movement. How might you convey happiness, sunshine, or heat? With bright eyes and an upturned face? With sprightly jumps? Silky-smooth arm swaying? Now develop movements that come from your ear. They don't have to stop there; your ear is merely the impetus. You might rise from the floor, leading with the right side of your head, then run in a huge figure eight. Try to integrate both elements as you create your dance. Keep it short and simple, concentrating on the emotions, textures, actions, and ideas that have to do with yellow and your right ear. Make clear choices, and don't hesitate to edit and refine. Show your dance

**Jen** *Body work is important because you can't act if there's tension in your body. It's debilitating to your work. You have to be free to receive impulses. Lots of people live in their heads rather than their bodies.*

to someone and see if your movement expresses what you think it does. See Avant-garde Theater: What Is It?, page 96.

# Posture

Stand up straight! Yeah, yeah. You may get tired of being told not to slouch, but if you don't get your posture in line, you will carry loads of unnecessary tension in your spine and be unable to move easily and efficiently—a big problem for an actor. Good posture, or alignment, doesn't mean standing ramrod straight like a soldier at attention, with your shoulder blades shoved together, knees locked, and neck rigid. It means standing tall, with a naturally elongated spine, an open—not clenched—upper back, and a long, supple neck.

Take a look at this drawing of a human skeleton in profile. Or, if you have one of those neat skeleton-assembly kits, study your handiwork—assuming you've assembled it correctly! Notice how the spinal column is not a straight up-and-down line running from the base of the skull to the tailbone. Rather, it has gentle contours, known as cervical (neck) and lumbar (lower spine) curves, which form a soft **S** shape. The skull balances comfortably on top. **Think of yourself as a marionette.** The string at the top of your skull pulls you upward, while the rest of your body hangs easily.

## FACE IT!

Take a yawning break. A yawn is one of the best stretching exercises you can do for your face, and your face is a remarkable and highly sensitive beeline to your character's innermost feelings. Unless the role demands it, actors never want to have a poker face (an impassive expression, revealing nothing of what a person is thinking or feeling). It's great if you're playing poker, but not so great if you're trying to convey emotions to an audience. Try watching people on the street—always a good lesson plan—and you'll get an eyeful of expressions. Happiness, pain, boredom, anxiety—each comes with an instantly recognizable facial feature: ear-to-ear grin, grimace, rolling eyes, furrowed brows.

Making faces is a great way to get your acting mask in working order. In acting, your face acts as a kind of mask—and is sometimes referred to as one—projecting and reflecting states of mind and emotions. The more mobile your mask, the more spontaneous and true to life your expressions will be. Think of Jim Carrey's amazingly plastic (mobile) features.

To get your mask working, you need to first loosen your muscles with a series of stretches. You can start with a yawn.

**Patrick** *Keep your back straight—posture is really important.*

Be at ease but alert, poised for action, ready to deliver a demanding monologue and move through space with grace and freedom. The less fuss you have to go through in terms of physical adjustments, the clearer your performance will be, unclouded by excess stress and strain.

Then:

**1.** Open your mouth wide.

**2.** Now squeeze your lips together, making your mouth as small as possible.

**3.** Turn those pursed lips into a huge smile; show off your teeth.

**4.** Get your tongue into the act by taking it on a tour of your mouth. Stick it out and try to touch your chin, then your nose.

**5.** Close your lips and move your mouth around.

**6.** Roll your eyeballs in a circle, then look up, down, side to side.

**7.** Now raise your eyebrows and lower them. Squeeze your eyes shut tight.

**8.** Finally, place your hands on your cheeks and head and massage your skin and scalp.

# chapter two

# Speak Up!

*Voice Warm-ups • Tongue Twisters •*
*Better Breathing • Voice Coaches • Projection •*
*Stage Whispers • Wacky Accents*

Ahem! There are so many ways to use your voice. You can make it loud or soft, deep or high, angry or soothing. The differences are significant. A booming voice commands your audience's immediate attention. A timid, barely audible squeak sets them on edge as they try to catch every word, while a rambling monotone might very well put them to sleep. Though there are differences in how you use your voice when you're performing on a stage or speaking into an ultrasensitive microphone on a film set, both require a voice that communicates with expression.

**Breathe In, Breathe Out** It all has to do with breathing. You pull the air into your lungs, then push it out, over and over again. Sounds simple enough. Becoming aware of your breathing and getting control of how you breathe are key to speaking and singing effectively onstage. These can be achieved through training that can help you overcome any number of problems and bad habits that you might have with your natural voice, including a hard-to-understand accent and a tendency to speak in a singsong rhythm. As an actor you want to be able to choose how your voice sounds and use it to its fullest capabilities.

What you know as your voice is really the result of four intricately connected pieces.

**1. Respiration:** breathing, moving air into and out of your lungs

**2. Phonation:** the process of producing sound as air passes from your lungs through the larynx (voice box), just behind the Adam's apple

**3. Resonation:** how the sound produced by your voice box is made louder; you have resonators (open spaces that work as amplifiers) in your chest cavity, your mouth, and your nose and sinus cavities

**4. Articulation:** how the sounds are shaped into recognizable words; your articulators are your lips, teeth, tongue, hard and soft palates, lower jaw, and uvula—that wiggly thing hanging down at the very back of your throat

**Find Your Diaphragm** Here's a simple, two-part breathing experiment. Part one: Strike up a casual conversation with a friend—about the weather, school, whatever. As you're talking, put one hand on your stomach and the other

**Jen** *I had no idea how important voice work is until I went to London to train. All of your emotions, instincts, and impulses come from your diaphragm. I saw Peter O'Toole onstage in London, in* Jeffrey Bernard Is Unwell. *He did entire speeches in one breath. It was just amazing.*

on your chest. You'll notice that when you inhale, your stomach contracts and your chest expands, sending tiny waves of tension up through your shoulders and throat. This little bit of gripping—barely noticeable during a calm chat—causes strain when you try to **project** your voice across a stage. (See Projection, page 18.)

Part two: Do a bunch of jumping jacks. Stop when you start to pant hard. Once again, put one hand on your stomach and the other on your chest. Something is different. This time, it's your stomach that is expanding—like a giant bellows—while your chest, shoulders, and neck stay relatively calm. You are breathing from your diaphragm, the big muscle that runs between your abdomen and chest. This is the most efficient form of breathing: your body's way of moving lots of air into and out of your lungs. Once you become accustomed to breathing this way —and you don't need to be gulping for air to do so— you'll find your voice is more relaxed and has more sensitivity, power, and flexibility.

Since your voice is an especially delicate instrument, it's best to exercise it daily, for just ten to twenty minutes, rather than infrequently for longer stretches. Following are a few exercises that you should try to do every day.

**project** [pro-JECT]: to send your voice through space with quality as well as volume

**David** *I think voice classes with the right teacher are very valuable. A teacher has excellent material, and can analyze and train your voice. One exercise I like is singing "Mommy made me mash my M&Ms" on a series of notes, going up the scale.*

**Good Vibrations** Time to get your lips into the act. Lying on your back, close your lips while keeping your teeth slightly apart. Lips together, teeth apart. Breathing slowly and deeply (see Make like a Bellows, below), relax your throat and jaw and allow a gentle hummmmm to move forward through your head to your lips. Your face is going to tickle! Keeping this forward sensation going, use your lips to make *mee, maaa, maar, maal* sounds. You'll have to part your lips a bit to let these sounds out.

**Tongue Stretch** This exercise gives you a sense of how to relax and open your throat so the vowel sounds (A, E, I, O, U) can travel freely from your vocal chords to your resonators. Sounds can literally get stuck in your throat or way back  in your mouth, giving your voice that annoyingly whiny, nasal quality. Sit up tall with your legs comfortably crossed. Open your mouth slightly as you place the tip of your tongue against the inside top of your lower teeth. Then push your tongue out between your upper and lower teeth until you feel a stretch at your tongue's root. Don't worry, it's securely attached. Once you've stretched, run through the vowels and feel how easily the sounds bounce around the inside of your mouth.

**Make like a Bellows** This exercise helps you learn to breathe from your diaphragm. Place this book on the floor and lie down next to it on your back with your legs and arms comfortably extended. Concentrate on your breathing as you feel your weight sink into the floor. After a moment or two, your body should feel like pudding. Pick up *Break a Leg!* and set it (gently!) on your stomach. Feel it lift and lower as you inhale and exhale. Slowly, deeply. Now it's time to vocalize. As you exhale, make an *ahhhh* sound. Don't say "ahhhh" with your mouth. Allow it to come flowing out from the bottom of your rib cage along with your breath. Congratulations! You are breathing from your diaphragm.

**Sound Off** Here's an exercise to get your consonants (all the sounds other than vowels) in shape. There are basically two types of consonant sounds. The first are the **explosives,** made when the air is stopped, then released along with the sound. Put your fingers in front of your lips as you say *p, t, k,* and *ch.* Feel the little jet of air that shoots out of your mouth. Now try *b, d,* and *g.* You still get a burst, but softer.

**Continuants** are consonant sounds accompanied by breath. When you say *m, n,* and *ng,* air is blocked by your lips or tongue but passes through your nose. When you say *l* and *r,* the tip of your tongue creates a tiny roadblock for the air passing between your lips. Other continuants come in pairs: breathed and voiced. The *th* sound in the word "thistle" is breathed; the same pair of letters in the word "those" is voiced—a sound comes along with the breath. Now try pairing *f* (breathed) and *v* (voiced) and *ss* (breathed) and *zz* (voiced).

**Bubble Gum** Right about now you're probably ready for some virtual bubble gum. Stick an imaginary piece in your mouth and chomp away. Add a voice to go with your chewing. Mmmmmmmmmmmm. Stick in another, and a third. Hey, might as well pop in the entire pack. Keep those sounds coming as you work the muscles in your face and tongue. Just because your mouth is closed doesn't mean you can't have a big, loud voice. Feel the tingle in your lips? Now relax your face (you've spit out the gum) and gently blow, keeping your lips lightly pressed together. You can tell that the flow of air coming out is steady because your lips tremble.

**Tongue Twisters** What's the point of tying your tongue up in knots? Tongue twisters not only limber up your mind; they are great practice for e-nun-ci-at-ing those vowels and consonants that you've been working on. Recite the three below slowly first, so you can get your tongue around every sound. Then try again faster. See if you can get through without fumbling or losing your articulation.

Peter Piper picked a peck of pickled peppers.
Did Peter Piper pick a peck of pickled peppers?
If Peter Piper picked a peck of pickled peppers,
Where's the peck of pickled peppers Peter Piper picked?

A tree-toad loved a she-toad
Who lived up in a tree.
He was a two-toed tree-toad,
But a three-toed toad was she.
The two-toed tree-toad tried to win
The three-toed she-toad's heart,
For the two-toed tree-toad loved the ground

That the three-toed tree-toad trod.

But the two-toed tree-toad tried in vain;

He couldn't please her whim.

From her tree-toad bower,

With her three-toed power,

The she-toad vetoed him.

A skunk sat on a stump and thunk the stump stunk,

but the stump thunk the skunk stunk.

Now hang in for one more, adding movement that corresponds to the rhythm of the words, goofy though it may be. Why connect words and movement? Because in acting, your voice and body function as a unit. What sorts of movements suggest themselves in the following tongue twister? Stomping? Bouncing? Skipping? Shifting your weight from side to side?

★ **Joey**  *Tongue twisters are helpful for your diction and your speech because you have to say each syllable clearly or you can't be understood.*

Mr. See owned a saw.

And Mr. Soar owned a seesaw.

Now, See's saw sawed Soar's seesaw

Before Soar saw See,

Which made Soar sore.

Had Soar seen See's saw

Before See sawed Soar's seesaw,

See's saw would not have sawed

Soar's seesaw.

So See's saw sawed Soar's seesaw.

But it was sad to see Soar so sore

Just because See's saw sawed

Soar's seesaw.

# Putting Your Voice to Work

You know how irritating it can be to listen to people speak in a monotone, a humdrum voice with virtually no expression. Their words sound flat and dull, and-it-can-be-dif-fi-cult-to-stay-in-ter-est-ed-in-what-they-are-say-ing —a definite negative for an actor. Fortunately, you can control and vary your tone of voice through a combination of stress, pitch, rhythm, diction, and quality. An understanding of how these variations can help your voice be more expressive will come in handy when you mark a script (see page 105).

**1. Stress:** the way you emphasize words or phrases, which affects their meaning

**2. Pitch:** how high or low your voice is

**3. Volume:** how loudly or softly you are speaking

**4. Rhythm:** how quickly or slowly you speak (long or short sounds and silences can drastically alter the meaning and musicality of speech)

**5. Diction:** how clearly you pronounce words; also called **articulation** and **enunciation**

**6. Quality:** the way your voice sounds; for example, raspy, nasal, breathy, or rich

If you've ever looked at a musical score, you know that the way the music is written indicates not only which notes are stressed and whether they are high or low (their pitch), but also their volume and rhythm: how loudly or softly and quickly or slowly they are to be played. Listen to people speaking and take note of how the stresses, pitch, volume, rhythms,

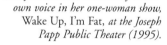

*Camryn Manheim relied solely on her own voice in her one-woman show,* Wake Up, I'm Fat, *at the Joseph Papp Public Theater (1995).*

and articulation of their words change according to their age, gender, mood, state of mind, and what they are saying. If someone is anxious, his or her words may veer all over the place: high to low and back, loud to louder, rapid to slow. Someone else, equally anxious, may speak in a barely audible rumble.

Read each of the following sentences out loud. The first time through, STRESS the words that are in capital letters. Notice how the different stresses change the meaning of the sentence.

If I've told you ONCE, I've told you a THOUSAND times.
IF I've TOLD you once, I've TOLD you a THOUSAND TIMES.
If I'VE TOLD YOU once, I'VE TOLD YOU a thousand times.

Now read them again, raising or lowering your pitch according to the way the words are arranged on the page.

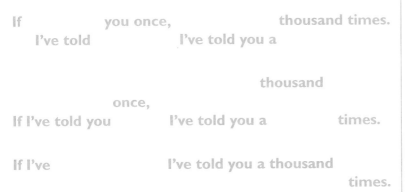

*An expressive voice makes your body language more effective.*

Notice how changes in pitch can make you seem perturbed, calm, agitated, frightened, angry, decisive, or wishy-washy. Try them yet again, changing first the volume, then the rhythm, diction, and quality of your voice. Read them out loud to a partner and see if his or her interpretation matches your own.

# Projection

**P**art of training your voice for the stage is learning how to make it BIG and FULL so that it can travel all the way to the very last row in the audience. One way, a wrong way, is to scream every word. Not only is this inefficient, it is irritating—to your fellow actors and to your audience. Most of us wouldn't choose to endure two hours of shouting if we didn't have to. Your goal is to project your voice without harming your vocal chords. Imagine your voice as a projectile missile, soaring toward its goal. A commanding voice doesn't need a large body to project it. Think of the actor Al Pacino, a relatively small person with an undeniably big voice.

Projection is not simply about making your voice loud enough to be heard; it is also about an active communication with the audience. If you're really tuned in, you'll be able to project your performance while sensing and responding to the audience's energy. You do this through a combination of breathing and voice techniques, an understanding of your character and his or her relationship to others in the play, and by scaling your performance to include the audience, even if you're not yet in the theater. If you wait too long to

> **Stephanie** *You have to use your vocal chords the right way. You have to learn to talk louder without straining by using your breath. If you don't project your voice at an audition, they won't pick you.*

expand your performance beyond the immediate action at hand—getting your part down pat—you'll find it difficult to adjust your voice and the scale of your performance when you move from the rehearsal studio into the theater.

Try this exercise. Pick a spot right next to you. Pick another in the middle distance, maybe halfway across the room. And find a third all the way across the room. Try to *place* your voice at each of these points without raising your volume. Use *intention,* your desire to place your voice, and *focus,* where you want it to go.

**Voice Tips:**

★ Be an active listener

★ Control your breathing

★ Pace yourself

★ Enunciate: e-nun-ci-ate

★ Collect and practice accents

# Shout It Out

If a role requires that you yell or scream, put your all-powerful diaphragm to work. The more air you supply to your voice, the greater sound you can achieve. Remember the bellows image. Relax your jaw and open your throat so that the sounds can flow out of your mouth. Use the vowels to carry the tone, and the consonants to keep your words clear. "NO, I DO NoT wanT To GO!" Think of sending your voice to the very back row of the audience. Don't force it; instead, concentrate on the energy and emotion of the words. If nerves are making you rush, not only will your diction suffer, you might become shrill and incapable of sustaining the proper volume. Even though your character is angry or distraught, you must try to stay calm and recite your lines as rehearsed, without adding all sorts of odd pauses or stops or running-together-of-words that will muddy your delivery. And keep breathing.

# Movies Worth a Listen

**B**elow are a number of films that feature actors trying on accents: regional American, foreign, and entirely invented. No doubt you'll come up with several more on your own.

★ American Actors Who Have Gone South

**Natalie Portman,** as a Kentucky teen in *Where the Heart Is* (2000)

**Robert De Niro,** as a North Carolina navy master chief in *Men of Honor* (2000)

**Matt Damon and Will Smith,** as a struggling golfer and his caddie in Georgia, in *The Legend of Bagger Vance* (2000)

★ American Actors Who Have Dived into Foreign Accents with Relish

**Meryl Streep,** as the Polish heroine of *Sophie's Choice* (1982) and as the Danish writer Isak Dinesen in *Out of Africa* (1985)

*Comedian Martin Short is known for his ability to create hilarious accents.*

**Taye Diggs,** as a Jamaican named Winston Shakespeare in *How Stella Got Her Groove Back* (2000)

**Gwyneth Paltrow,** as the Bard's English sweetheart in *Shakespeare in Love* (1998)

**Loretta Young,** as the Swedish heroine of *The Farmer's Daughter* (1947)

**Irene Dunne,** as England's Queen Victoria in *The Mudlark* (1950) and as a Norwegian immigrant living in San Francisco in *I Remember Mama* (1948)

**Frank Sinatra,** as a Spaniard in *The Pride and the Passion* (1957)

**Marlon Brando,** as an English Marc Antony in *Julius Caesar* (1953); he used approximately the same accent when he played the French emperor Napoleon in *Desirée* (1954)

★ Foreign Actors Doing American Accents

**Australian Mel Gibson,** as a loose-cannon cop in all of the *Lethal Weapon* movies and as a reluctant Revolutionary War hero in *The Patriot* (2000)

**Fellow Aussie Russell Crowe,** as a heroic whistle-blower in *The Insider* (1999)

**English actress Emma Thompson,** as Susan Stanton in *Primary Colors* (1998)

**English actor Gary Oldman,** as Lee Harvey Oswald in *JFK* (1991)

**English actor Laurence
Olivier, as a terrifying Nazi
dentist in *Marathon Man*
(1976)**

**English actor Gary Oldman,
as a chilling Russian terrorist
in *Air Force One* (1997)**

**Peter Sellers, a master at
phony accents, invented the
ludicrous French accent of
Inspector Clouseau, which he
used in all of the *Pink Panther*
movies.**

**The four Marx Brothers, all
born in New York City, had
distinct onscreen personalities.
Groucho and Zeppo spoke as
they normally did offscreen,
Harpo never spoke at all, and
Chico used a thick, ridiculous
Italian accent.**

**Canadian Mike Myers plays an
Englishman, a Scot, and a certain evil doctor whose origins
are considerably harder to pin
down in the second *Austin
Powers* (1999).**

**American Sean Penn originated
the now-ubiquitous Surfer
Dude accent in *Fast Times
at Ridgemont High* (1982).**

**Canadian Martin Short, as
Franck the wedding planner
with the superconvoluted
accent in *Father of the Bride*
(1991)**

**Tony Curtis's Bronx, New
York, accent gets hilariously
in the way in his role as an
English knight in the Middle
Ages in *The Black Shield of
Falworth* (1954): "Yonda lies
da castle of my fodda."
Translation: Yonder lies the
castle of my father.**

*American actress Gwyneth
Paltrow mastered a British
accent in* Shakespeare in
Love (*1998*).

# Stage Whispers

It's 4 A.M. A pale shaft of moonlight streaming through an open window illuminates your path as you, a world-famous private eye, slink along the hallway of an old mansion, searching for a hidden key. The owners of the house are sound asleep. At least you thought they were. "Shhhhh," you whisper to your jittery assistant, who has just bumped into an umbrella stand. "I think I hear someone coming!" The audience breaks out in goose bumps. Hey, wait a minute. If you're whispering, how can anyone beyond the first row hear what you're saying? Because you aren't really whispering. You're creating the impression of a whisper through your body language, facial expression, and tone of voice. You might be creeping along on tiptoe, hunched over, with your eyebrows raised and a finger to your lips. But the words coming out of your mouth can be heard by everyone in the audience.

For inspiration, think of how a little kid acts out a whisper. He or she mimics the raised eyebrows and the finger to the lips, but the voice that comes out is anything but hushed. There's a little—or maybe a lot—of "voice," or phonation, in the whisper. This is the idea behind a stage whisper. **Play with different sounds,** using a little bit of voice, to see which are most effective. Keep your consonants clear. Try both a high and raspy hiss and a low, velvety rumble. You'll find that you can be quite loud and still project the feeling of a whisper. Audiences are eager to suspend their belief and participate in the illusion. If you believe in your whisper, they will, too.

Now, about that key . . .

# Accents

In the musical *My Fair Lady*, Professor Henry Higgins (who spends his time studying how people speak) comes across the poor flower-seller Eliza Dolittle. Her working-class accent, known as Cockney, offends his upper-class ears. Henry Higgins obviously doesn't appreciate how Eliza shapes her vowels and consonants, and he isn't at all interested in the variety of her speech. But you are. And you'd want to be able to answer her if she were to ask you, "'OW AW yuh, dAWlin?" (Translation: How are you, darling?) Actors make a habit of listening and mimicking—politely and discreetly—so when they land a role that requires them to speak with an accent other than their own, they will get it right.

Every language—and there are more than 4,000 around the world—has its own sounds and rhythms. And within each of those languages are unique regional accents: the distinct way that words are pronounced. Take a quick tour with the list below.

*Will Smith and Matt Damon take on southern accents in* The Legend of Bagger Vance (*2000).*

**1.** When an English-speaking Parisian says, "I have a ticket to the zoo," the sentence rolls along with a notable sound: "I yav a tEEkit to ze zu."

**2.** The same words recited by a Venetian have a different, equally romantic pitch and rhythm: "Aya 'av a (like "e" in let) tEEkit to da dzoo."

**3.** While a Berliner might very well say: "I half ah teeket to zeh ZOO."

**4.** And when you hear them from the mouth of a southern American, you'll get another earful entirely: "Ah hAeve aw tee-iket to the zew."

It's fun to try on different accents with the same sentence. Some are filled with growls and sudden stops and starts that happen way back in your throat. Others will strike you as incredibly musical; you practically sing as the words trickle off of your tongue.

Most American actors usually speak with, or have been coached to speak with, what is known as a Standard American English accent, which means they speak without a trace of regionalism. In other words, even though they might have grown up in the Deep South, the Northeast, or the Midwest, their accents don't give away their roots. This doesn't mean they don't relish the opportunity to try on an accent from some exotic locale or even from somewhere relatively close to home.

*Mike Myers mimics a slew of accents in the* Austin Powers *movies.*

Unless you are familiar with your character's language or region, acquaint yourself through listening and imitating and, if possible, conversations with a native speaker. Get hold of beginning-level language tapes so you become accustomed to the sound of the language itself. You'll learn some of it in the process, which is always a good thing. Rent movies that feature an actor speaking English with your character's accent. (See Movies Worth a Listen, pages 20–21.) Be sure to keep your character's age and level of education in mind as you search. These factors affect how you approach creating the accent. The film and language departments of your library, your local video store, and the Web will also be able to guide you.

**Record yourself speaking with your new accent.** Listen carefully. How do you sound? You'll be amused at first. Drill yourself and record and listen again. Don't worry about mastering every nuance. You want your words to be understood, so your accent will not need to be heavy. You will pick out the key sounds, rhythms, and stresses so that you communicate the essence of your character's origins. Once you feel fairly confident, give your new accent a whirl in the real world. Go into a store and ask for directions to the nearest bus stop. If you get a snicker or a look of bewilderment, you know you have a bit more work to do.

# I Need a Coach!

There are all sorts of reasons to seek help from a voice coach. Maybe you run out of breath when speaking or have trouble projecting with volume and authority. Your voice may be a bit whiny or singsong, or have a definite nasal twang that limits the parts you can go for. Or you may have landed a role that requires you to speak with an especially hard-to-master foreign accent—and your eager attempts to soak it up through movies, conversations with native speakers, and language tapes just aren't doing the trick. A good voice coach can help with all of the above. Don't just grab the nearest yellow pages. You want to be certain your coach has proper credentials and lots of experience working with actors. Ask your teachers and fellow actors for recommendations.

**David** *I've done an English accent and fooled around with others. I've tried a light Spanish accent because I had to sing for a Spanish radio show. Listen to people who actually have the accent if you have a coach who isn't terribly good at accents.*

**Joey** *Accents are a lot of fun. I had to learn Italian, Brooklyn, and English accents. I went to a speech coach and listened to tapes, which really helped. Once you get into the mood, it's pretty easy.*

**Jen** *I enjoy doing accents. They're easy for me to pick up. For some plays you need to have them. With something like Tennessee Williams, you have to have that southern accent.*

⭐ **David** *My coach is an actress herself. I go over monologues with her. She knows all of the tips and tricks of the business.*

⭐ **Evynne** *My new coach told me that when you're singing in a quiet voice, no one in the back of the room can hear you. I got louder and louder until I could finally sing at my full voice.*

⭐ **Joey** *Have a good attitude about the business, and use your coach as a resource. If you have questions, don't be too shy to ask.*

⭐ **Jen** *Coaches serve a different purpose from a teacher. They're excellent for helping you with monologues, but the majority of scenes are written for several people. You learn from watching others.*

# Frog in Your Throat?

If you have ever cheered for hours at a football game, you know what it means to wake up with a hoarse, croaky voice. Actors who use their voices incorrectly—because of uncontrolled yelling, improper breathing, speaking at too high or too low a pitch—can end up with a nasty case of laryngitis, an uncomfortable swelling in the throat, or even small growths (nodes) on their vocal chords. The best way to avoid these unpleasantries is to practice the correct voice techniques. Remember, your voice, just like your body, is an instrument that requires care. Abuse it and you will eventually have problems. If you do have a problem, you must see a doctor. Once you recover you may want to take preventive measures and get help from a voice coach or speech-language pathologist. Think of it as vocal insurance.

# chapter three

# Theater Games and Improvisation

**Name Game • Memory Walking Game • Freezing Game • Sense & Confidence Boosters • Structured & Unstructured Improvs • Partnered Mirroring**

Grab a few friends or relatives to form a cast. Theater games and improvs, as they're known, are a great way to increase your many powers of observation and awareness and build a sense of involvement and camaraderie. They also increase your sense of presence, of being in the moment, when you are aware of and open to your surroundings.

*Charlie Chaplin (far right) and pals take a spill in* The Rink *(1916).*

**observation:** the act of looking closely at people and the environment to enhance your acting work

**motivation:** the reasons behind a character's actions or behavior

Improvs, which are especially fun because you get to make stuff up as you go along, are also used to develop new material and explore unknown facets of an existing character. Sometimes a director resolves problems with a difficult scene by having the actors put aside their scripts for a while and improvise using their own words. By breaking away from the script, they often can get to the core of the emotions that are the **motivation** behind their characters' behavior: why they do what they do.

Sometimes improvs are structured, which means that you have a problem, a set of circumstances, or a prop to improvise around. Sometimes they're totally free-form: you create a scene from scratch. This means that you establish the who, what, where, and why on the fly, as you're improvising. Either way, it's essential to be alert to every move and sound, and set your imagination in high gear. The following exercises are designed to prime you for this high-energy spontaneity and awareness.

# Games to Get Things Rolling

Name Game. This game gets your memory up and running and is a great way to create a sense of cast bonding. You can't help but feel like a tiny community after reciting one another's names over and over again! Stand in a circle about an arm's length from one another. One person starts the game (let's say it's your little sister) by clapping her hands together with a sliding motion that ends with one hand reaching toward another member of the circle. As she claps, she says your name and directs her hand, voice, and eyes toward you. Eye contact is key. You respond by naming someone else in your circle and directing your clap, voice, and eyes toward that person. And so it goes. The idea is to respond as quickly as you can, keeping the "conversation" going strong. Don't think about what you're doing. Just react. Once you get the rhythm down, shake out your hands and make a smaller circle, almost shoulder to shoulder, and try the game even faster. Keep your motions, voice, and eye contact sharp.

**Memory Walking Game.** Have you ever played a memory game with cards? The one where you try to remember the positions of the matching pairs as you flip the cards faceup? Here's one you play with your body. The ability to remember a series of directions comes in handy when you start working on blocking (page 98).

**Molly**  *If a director says, "Okay, I want you to pretend that you've just come home from school and your brother is lying on the floor and he's really hurt," you have to be able to pretend that he's actually there. Or if you are supposed to be in a beautiful place, you have to make the audience believe you are really there. You might look around and be amazed at what you see.*

**Joey**  *Improvs are lots of fun. Lots of times things can go wrong when you're performing and you have to think quickly. Improvs help you deal with those situations. Improvs are also useful for group work.*

**Jen**  *I love improv. It's another one of those things that I do naturally. Improvs help you learn how to act on impulse. Some people hold themselves back. Don't be afraid to look really stupid.*

Everyone lines up at one end of the room, except for the designated leader, who calls out instructions for a walking pattern. For example: "Take six steps forward. Now make a quarter turn to your right and take three steps backward. Make a half turn to your left and take five steps forward. Now take eight steps backward and make a quarter turn to your left. Take six steps forward and make a half turn to your right. Are you back where you started? You should be." Don't attempt the entire pattern the first few times through. The leader should start calling out one command at a time, waiting for everyone to complete the action before going on. The second time, he or she gives a few commands at once. The trick is to listen very carefully to each command as you file it in your memory. You'll find that after a few run-throughs you'll be able to remember an entire series of commands. The leader should feel free to change around directions and numbers of steps to create interesting patterns and memory challenges. If your group is really amazing, try the game with everyone's eyes closed. Just be careful you don't have people crashing into things.

**Freezing Game.** Here's a chance to use your active imagination and quicksilver reflexes. You'll also get a taste of character work. Spread out so you have plenty of room to move. Pick one person, a.k.a. the sorcerer, to call out the commands and questions. You'll all get a chance. Here goes. "Poof! You're a beetle scurrying across a muddy road in the countryside." You all transform yourselves into determined little bugs, noses to the ground. You know *all* about that beetle that you've become. (Observation bank! See page 73.) "Freeze!" shouts the sorcerer, and marches up to each of you with a series of beetle-relevant questions, such as "Is there a car coming?" "How far away is your nest?" Or "Are you searching for food?" "Are your legs cold?" You know the answers almost without thinking. Another "Poof!" and you've become bolts of lightning, striking rooftops in a small town. You jump and dart around the room with electric intensity. "Freeze!" "What is the name of the town?" "What season is it?" "Did you start any fires?" The game can go in just about any direction. Try being animals, people, forces of nature. Be as convincing in your story as you are in your body language.

**Playing for Real:**

★ Be in the moment

★ Find your motivation

★ Let your imagination run wild

★ Respond to your fellow actors

# Improvs

**Sit, Stand, and Lean.** This structured improv for three quick-witted people is like a superchallenging game of musical chairs. Its structure is simple: at all times, one of you must be sitting, one standing, and the third leaning against the back of a chair. And you have to keep talking and continuously changing your positions. The first thing is to invent a scenario. Who are the three of you, where are you, and what are you talking about? Could be you're teenagers in the school lunchroom discussing a recent rock concert—probably not a huge stretch of the imagination. Or maybe you're eminent astronomers at a high-powered conference hashing out a new theory of the universe. Once you've decided who, where, and what, grab a chair and place it in the middle of the room. Start the game with each of you in one of the positions. It might be helpful to have someone else say "Go!" Teamwork is crucial. Not only do you have to establish your character and keep up an intelligent conversation, you have to pay close attention to your partners' movements so you don't end up sitting in someone's lap, knocking over the chair, or crashing into one another.

## IMPROV TROUPES

Some actors love to improvise so much that they make a profession out of it. Here are a few of the better-known improv troupes. Check out their Web sites, below. You might also take a look at www.improvamerica.com, which has tons of info.

**GROUNDLINGS** Named after the poorer members of the audience during Shakespeare's day who sat or stood on the ground rather than sitting in the more exclusive bleachers; see Time Out for Shakespeare, page 129. www.groundlings.com

**SECOND CITY** This troupe (see photo above) spawned many well-known actors. You've probably heard of SCTV (Second City TV): John Candy, Harold Ramis, Martin Short, and Rick Moranis were among the original members. www.secondcity.com

**SPOLIN PLAYERS** Named after Viola Spolin, a creator of theater games and exercises that are still in use. www.spolin.com/players.html

**Flying Without a Net.** Now that you've sampled a structured improvisation, you'll want to try an unstructured improv, without a framework on which to build. Of course, as soon as someone makes the first move, each of you will have strong feelings about what the scene should be about, not to mention how it should unfold. As long as you stay extra attentive to one another's actions and words and open to possibilities, you'll have fun. Cooperation and flexibility are key.

One of you will have to start. Give everyone a turn to begin. If it's you, be sure you quickly map out at least the beginnings of an idea in your head. If your actions are muddy, your partners will not know how to respond. Let's say you jump into this improv with the idea of building a sand castle at the beach. You start by kneeling and making the motions of digging and patting sand into the shape of a turret. Your partners quickly catch on. One starts digging a moat and another

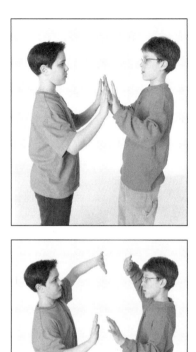

begins to mold a fearsome dragon. Maybe you collaborate on a bridge. You don't know how it's going to "look" until it's complete. The joy is in the making. If you come up with some really terrific results, make careful notes. You may have the beginnings of a script!

See Sensory Perception, page 81, for improvs you can do on your own.

**Mirroring,** or copying, a partner's movement is a great way to refine your all-important observation skills. The first step is to find a partner. Try a brother, sister, or friend. Someone relatively close to your own size would be ideal. Stand facing each other; close enough to maintain good eye contact. Once you decide which of you is the leader, that person will initiate slow, supersmooth movements that the other will mirror. Don't rush or lag behind your partner. The idea is for the two of you to move as one. After a while, you'll find it easy to work in unison.

# chapter four

# Getting Physical

*Miming • Clowning • Juggling • Stand-up Comedy •
Stage Combat • Falling • Fainting • Stunts • Tap Dancing •
Musical Theater • Fake Kissing • Death Scenes*

Y ou've seen actors whose actions seem to speak louder than their words. Something magical—or utterly ridiculous—happens every time they gesture or take a step. In acting, you need to get to know your body and put it to work. Not only will it get you from here to there; if properly tuned, it will do so with great style and expression.

*Flying through the air with the greatest of ease, these guys train to be stuntmen.*

*happiness*

*sadness*

# Mime

The art of mime is an ancient physical form based on the silent dialogue between a performer and audience, and it's a wonderful way for an actor to learn how to use his or her face and body fully and expressively. Because there are no words to distract from the activity at hand, actors quickly learn how their bodies respond to weight, mass, and texture. You may have seen classic mime routines like tugging on an imaginary rope, climbing an invisible ladder, or riding up and down in a phantom elevator. Each of these illusions involves carefully chosen gestures and movements that clearly communicate an action and establish the "existence" or placement of imaginary props. Mime also involves a lot of improvisation. If you've played charades, you know how important it is that your gestures be crystal clear and that you be able to switch gears at a moment's notice.

Mime uses classic facial expressions to convey five basic emotions: **happiness, sadness, fear, surprise, and anger.** Though you know each expression well, it's a good idea to practice in front of a mirror until you feel you've internalized each one. Take note of each feature and how it relates to the others. What are your eyebrows doing when you frown? How

*fear*

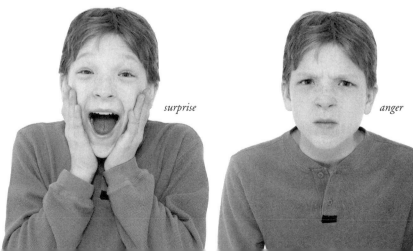

*surprise*

*anger*

about your mouth? How is a sad face different from an angry one? How is it the same? Are your eyes animated, too? You've heard that your eyes are the mirror of your soul. If they're glazed over or wandering, the expression will look odd and won't project the emotion to your audience.

Think of an activity you do regularly. It doesn't have to be anything fancy. Try brushing your teeth. You need to use your gestures to establish "props" like a sink, running water, a toothbrush, toothpaste, maybe a cup, and of course you already have your body and your teeth. Next run through the familiar motions as you recall them. You might find that as you improvise you're adding extras or leaving out essentials. **Don't exaggerate your movements.** Just be precise. The audience needs to "see" what you see. Mime is all about communicating the gist, or essence, of an action, an essential skill for an actor. Now, with your face at its elastic best, try running through the classic mime routines below.

**David**  *I think mime is important because you need to make your actions as well as your words clear onstage. A dramatic monologue won't connect if you are just standing there stiff. Mime helps you to be aware of your gestures.*

# Classics Guaranteed to Wow

**Wall Warm-up** Stand in front of a full-length mirror and stretch your arms out in front of you, parallel to the floor with your palms pushing forward—like you're saying "Stop!" Press your hands flat against the mirror, first fingertips, then palms, keeping your arms stretched long. Worry about the smudges later. Your torso should be upright, not tilting forward or backward. Without changing a thing, take two steps back, away from the mirror. Do you still "feel" its flatness against your palms? Good! You're ready to bend reality with the Wall.

**Mime Tips:**

★ Fine-tune your facial expressions

★ Keep movements simple

★ Investigate imaginary spaces

★ Remember: silence is golden

**The Wall** Stand far enough from the mirror so you have room to move but can still check out your progress. Slowly and smoothly, place one hand, then the other, on the virtual wall in front of you. Try to recapture the flatness of the mirror. Keep your hands strong and solid. No mushy fingers. As you work, check your reflection to be sure your palms are truly flat and on the same spatial plane. You want to create the impression of a wall, not a jagged cliff. Now work your way down the "wall," one hand at a time, bending your knees and sinking into a crouch. Then travel up again, reaching way up on tiptoe. Creep to your right and left. (Imagine it's pitch black and you're groping along a fortress wall for a secret opening. You have only your hands to guide you.) Don't twist your wrists or push the heels of your hands too far forward. Think flat and solid.

Want to go around a corner? A piece of cake, once you establish the right angle that forms where two walls meet. Keep your left hand on the "wall" as you place your right hand on the "corner." Create a right angle with your fingers and palm. Now, without moving your feet, place your left hand on the corner, just above your right. You're hugging the corner. Lift your right hand and place it flat on the next "wall," the one around the "corner." Take a step forward, around the corner, with your right foot. Lift your left hand and place it next to your right. Bring your left foot next to your right. You've turned the corner!

**Play Ball** Now that you've conquered walls, try playing catch with an imaginary ball. This isn't any old ball. It is a magic, morphing object that changes size and weight. One minute it's small, light, and bouncy, the next it's lumpy and gigantic and weighs a ton. If you're working solo, toss the ball into the air and catch it, following its movement with your eyes and registering its impact with your body. If you don't "see" and "feel" the ball, your audience certainly won't either. When it's light, you hardly need to move to send it skyward; your arm and hand can do all the work. Flick those wrists. When it's heavy, you have to heave-ho to get it into the air and practically collapse as it comes crashing back into your arms. Ooooof! How do you demonstrate the ball's changing weight and mass? Try tossing it to a partner. This gets tricky. Each of you has to stay hyperaware and anticipate the other's moves so you can react appropriately to the ball's changing size and shape.

⭐ **Patrick** *Mime teaches you about isolations of the body and hand coordination. It takes a lot of practice to make it perfect.*

When you're ready to add another imaginary ingredient to your mime arsenal, try catching your ball inside a paper bag. "Hold" a "paper bag" with one hand (be sure to shape your palm and fingers to establish the size and shape of its bottom) and toss your ball into the air. As you catch it in the bag, snap the fingers on your free hand to simulate the sound of its landing. Play with this routine. You might reach high to catch it, or snare it low to the ground. You might even "miss" occasionally, and have to chase the ball down as it rolls away from you. If you happen to toss two balls into the air at once, do they land in your bag at the same split second? Probably not. You may want to incorporate this routine into your clowning (see page 40).

**Elevator Going Up! And Down!** Walk toward the "elevator," facing away, or upstage, from your audience. Reach to your side and press the Up or Down button. Remember to establish the solidity of the wall. Look up so you can "see" the floor numbers above the elevator. When the elevator arrives, watch the doors open, step inside, and turn around to face front. Watch the doors close and push the button for your floor. Now comes the fun part. If the elevator is going up, bend your knees a bit as it starts to move, then slowly straighten them as it rises. When it stops, lift onto your toes for a second. If it's going down, lift onto your toes as it starts to descend, lowering your heels slowly as it continues downward. As it stops, bend and straighten your knees to register the slight jolt of the car. When you reach your floor, watch the doors open and step out of the elevator.

# Clowning: You Don't Have to Run Away and Join the Circus

People have always loved to laugh. Clowns, also known as jesters or fools, held powerful positions in the ancient courts of the Far East, Rome, and Greece. The Elizabethans featured them in their dramas, and clowns amused Mexico's ferocious Aztec emperor Montezuma or else!

A basic knowledge of clowning is good for you if you're an actor because it teaches you all about rhythm and physical comedy—how a perfectly timed simple action, like giving someone a scathing look, can be amplified into something

# Neutral Mask

The great French mime Jacques Le Coq (1921–1999) was one of the masters of the modern-day use of what's known as a neutral mask. Le Coq believed that a mask can help you understand huge concepts like space, shape, movement, and energy as well as teach you how to use your own body—your primary tool as an actor—most efficiently, without a lot of extra fuss or flourishes. The mask is usually plain white, black, or brown, with holes for the eyes and nose only; the mouth is covered and always silent. If you'd like to make one, there's a simple pattern on page 171.

Rather than covering, or masking, your personality, think of a mask as somehow freeing you of your inhibitions. You don't have to worry about making a mistake. If your face is covered, no one knows it's you! Actually, they do, but the mask gives you license to explore without worrying about the impact of your own facial expressions. You know how difficult it is to maintain an impassive appearance, especially when you're trying hard not to smile or frown. Your audience concentrates on *what* you're doing rather than *who* you are.

Whether you make up your own simple routines or try the Classics on pages 37–40, there are a few things to remember to get the most out of mask work:

1.  Don't touch the mask; this is distracting.

2.  Keep your head up so the mask can be seen; this keeps the energy flowing outward.

3.  Don't talk or make sounds; even a squeal will break the spell.

4.  You can work solo in front of a full-length mirror or with a partner. Both ways are valuable and teach you different things.

5.  If you're working in front of a mirror, don't worry about how you look. You are "inside" the mask. Concentrate instead on your actions.

6.  Streamline your movement to bring it into sharper focus.

7.  If you're working with a partner, take turns being the mask wearer and the observer. Here's a chance to offer constructive criticism. Is your mask-wearing partner communicating purposefully and precisely? If not, how can he or she redirect or clarify the pantomime? Once you've had a chance to perform for each other, try a mask duet.

8.  Don't be tempted to talk. Your voice will be muffled by the mask, anyway.

Once you've explored some of the mask's potential, and are beginning to feel confident in your ability to tell a silent story with your body, it's time to bring your face back into the creative mix. You'll want to come back to the mask again and again to recharge your batteries.

## MARCEAU THE MAGNIFIQUE

Along with silent film stars Charlie Chaplin, Buster Keaton, Harry Langdon, and Stan Laurel and Oliver Hardy, Marcel Marceau is one of the world's most famous mimes. His character, Bip—a clown distinguished by his striped shirt, slightly too short black pants, and crumpled high hat—gets into all sorts of amusing mischief. Marceau has mimed for the movies, too. He plays a deaf and mute puppeteer *and* a mad scientist who speaks in the comedy *Shanks* (1974), and performs a brilliant cameo in Mel Brooks's hilarious *Silent Movie* (1976).

*Marcel Marceau as Bip the Clown*

outrageous. Like mime, clowning uses exaggerated gestures, and is usually performed in silence—unless you count the occasional obnoxious sound, like the blare of a horn. Unlike mime, it is informal and can be a bit rude.

Sight gags, pranks, pratfalls, somersaults, juggling, slow burns, stilt walking, and magic tricks are all part of any self-respecting clown's bag of high jinks. If you can do a handstand, a cartwheel, or a split, or stand on your head—great! Start with simple routines. As you gain skills and confidence, you can create increasingly elaborate skits. Remember, clowning is all in the timing.

**1.** Never rush.

**2.** Keep your gestures big, simple, and direct. Too much fussing will confuse your audience, especially the youngest members.

**3.** Concentrate on developing a few amusing mannerisms that define your character: a goofy walk or shrug; a habit of dropping things.

**4.** Just as you did with mime, practice your facial expressions in front of a mirror: happiness, sadness, anger, sorrow, and befuddlement are the basics.

Here are a few solo and duet skits that will give you a taste of clowning. Feel free to play with the routines or make up your own. Bear in mind that the repetition of an action develops your character and is funny to your audience.

The Trip This is a classic and easy pratfall. The gag is that there is a spot or something on the floor that is making you trip, over and over again.

**1.** Shake out your arms and legs so you're nice and relaxed. You're not in a hurry and you haven't a care in the world.

**2.** Take three normal-size steps forward. Step, two, three.

**3.** On the third step, hook your back foot behind the heel of your front foot and fall forward, landing on the foot that did the hooking. If you hook your left foot onto your right heel, you'll fall onto your left foot.

**4.** As you hook, make an expression that shows your surprise; let your arms respond, too.

**5.** Share your reaction with your audience.

**6.** Do the routine three times, always starting from the same place, making the trip bigger each time, until you actually fall down (see Falling, page 54).

**7.** Once you've fallen, get up, dust yourself off, and start all over again, only this time try to "trick" the tripping spot by taking a big step over or way around it.

**8.** Look at the spot. Try to "fix" it.

**9.** Look at your audience. Share your dilemma. You're going to conquer that spot. But of course, since you're a clown, you still trip and fall.

**10.** Keep your face actively involved. Your expressions as well as your actions grab the audience.

★ **Evynne** *Clowning teaches you that you can be funny when you're not even trying, and it frees you to be who you are.*

★ **Joey** *I like mime and clowning. I did a mime where I was driving a car and I suddenly stopped and hit this kid and kept on driving. Then I hit a few more. With clowning, there are lots of little things you can do, like the Trip and the Double Take. In clowning, they always say three is the magic number. The third time you do something, like the Trip, you make it huge and lose your temper and get furious at the floor.*

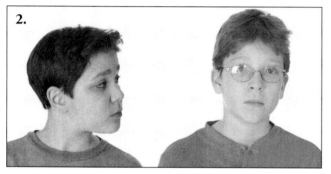

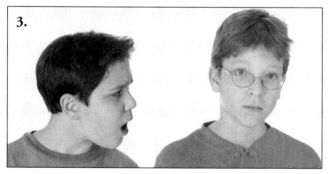

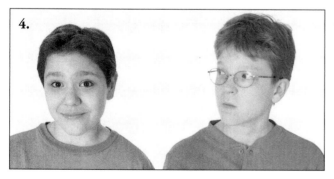

**Slow Burn** This entertaining gag is a classic with a wonderfully weird name. And it's a duet, so find a partner. You play the "straight man," your partner plays the "clown." Then you switch roles.

**1.** Stand next to each other, shoulder to shoulder, facing your audience.

**2.** Continue looking forward as your partner turns his head slowly to look at you, then returns to face front.

**3.** The instant your partner returns to face front, he does a rapid second look at you (called a **double take**) with a shocked expression and returns slowly to front, taking in the audience with his eyes. "Can you believe this person?" he seems to be saying.

**4.** Meanwhile, after his double take, you react with a **slow burn.** You are angry and have a fierce expression as you turn your head to glare at him, then take in the audience with wide eyes as you slowly return your face to the front. Feel the burn.

## Clown Wear

Once you've mastered a routine or twelve, you may feel the urge to suit up in full clown regalia. If the spirit moves you, go right ahead. You'll be quite a sight. Your local drugstore, especially around Halloween, and your dad's closet (ask first!) are good places to find gear like greasepaint (an old-fashioned stick makeup), a curly wig and nutty hat, a colorful shirt, huge pants with suspenders, pockets, and patches, and extra-jumbo floppy shoes. Come to think of it, you can make a pretty fine hat out of an old lampshade. Paint it a brilliant color, plop it on top of your wig, and you're set. You might even staple a crazy-looking flower to the top rim for an even jauntier effect.

## Clown Gear

There's a whole slew of props a clown might use: balloons, squirt bottles, a huge scarf, mirrors, gigantic sunglasses, an umbrella, boxing gloves, rubber snakes, an enormous sheriff's badge. You can find some of this stuff around the house, at your neighborhood drugstore, in catalogs, and on the Web (see Web Sites, page 212). Many are incredibly easy to make.

## Make a Clown Mobile

How about a silly clown car? No problem. Find a cardboard box that's big enough to step into—about 2 × 3 feet should be fine. Cut off the bottom and top and attach a pair of suspenders or staple two pieces of strong elastic (attach one end of each piece to the back and one to the front) so you can sling it over your shoulders. Paint it however you wish. Maybe it's a fire truck or a police car, or maybe it's a dune buggy.

### JUGGLING

Juggling is every clown's stock-in-trade, and contrary to popular opinion, it is not all that difficult. Some fancy juggling happens in these movies: *Abbott and Costello Meet the Mummy* (more funny than fancy); *Arabian Nights* (1942 version); *The Greatest Show on Earth* (1952 version); *The Juggler of Notre Dame* (1982 version); and *A Kid in King Arthur's Court* (1995).

# Comedy

**Stand-up** Do you like to stand in front of your friends and tell jokes or do impersonations of famous people? You're certainly not alone. Jim Carrey, Bette Midler, Chris Rock, Jerry Seinfeld, Chris Tucker, Robin Williams, Steve Martin, and Rosie O'Donnell, among many, many other actors do, too, and all of them started their performing careers doing comedy routines for whoever would listen. Eventually, they polished their acts enough to get dates in comedy clubs, where they sometimes bombed—hey, it's part of the stand-up learning curve—revised and reworked weak material, and eventually knocked 'em dead.

**Stand-ups are solo performers** who stand up in front of an audience, with just a microphone and maybe a few props for company. They memorize, and often make up, hundreds of jokes with, hopefully, great punch lines. This doesn't mean a bunch of knock-knock jokes. Stand-ups create routines packed with funny observations and comments about society, politics, fashion, whatever. They create Character Journals by the bucketload so that they can imitate famous people or make fun of stereotypes using a few carefully honed observations of speech patterns, expressions, or physical mannerisms. And they are superaware of their word choices and the rhythm of their delivery. A pause for effect in midsentence allows a certain word to sink in and get a laugh.

## THAT'S FUNNY?

There's no getting around the fact that some jokes are told at the expense of others. We've all done it. We pick an aspect of someone's appearance, speech, or behavior and make a funny/cruel remark that gets a laugh. Comedians do it all the time, and when they do we don't necessarily mind because they manage to do it in a way that is not mean-spirited. Even though they may be delivering a not-too-gentle poke in the ribs, they are not trying to hurt feelings. This, of course, takes great skill and perspective and is not recommended material for a beginner's routine.

Stand-up is a kind of hyperactive conversation that develops between the performer and the audience. It's great training for actors. The best stand-ups are fantastic improvisers with quicksilver timing, able to react and adjust to the audience's mood on a second's notice. Experienced stand-ups often can anticipate a joke's tanking and repair it on the fly. The performer delivers, the audience feeds back a response. Afterward, the performer assesses his or her routine. Did the audience laugh in all the right places? If not, the stand-up isn't discouraged. She dusts her ego off and takes a good, hard look at her material, fixes what she thinks went wrong, and tries it out again.

*Actor and talk-show host Chris Rock started out as a stand-up comedian.*

Stand-ups are constantly on the prowl for new material. If you'd like to be a stand-up, start a notebook and write down everything that tickles your funny bone. Keep your notes upbeat and kind. No cruel remarks about the way people look, talk, or dress. Instead, focus on silly stuff that happens at school, in your family, or on the street. There's a gold mine of material out there, just waiting for you to make a joke out of it. Hey, did you hear the one about . . .

# Stage Combat

**E**n garde! Put up your dukes! Thwap! Slam! Aaaaargh! Whether it's a fight to the finish between sword-wielding pirates, a messy barroom brawl, or a single, shocking slap to the face, skillfully choreographed stage combat adds exciting action and drama to a performance. But don't start swinging your fists willy-nilly or stabbing at your scene partner with a broom handle.

Stage combat tells a story through the illusion, and only the illusion, of violence. It is a masterful dance between you and your partner built on rules, trust, and timing. The first rule of stage combat is that the "victim," never the "aggressor," is always in control. The victim lets the aggressor know when he or she is ready for the move to begin. No one should get hurt because there should never be an opportunity for hurt to happen. If you do get too close and accidentally injure your partner, he or she will flinch from then on. And the illusion you're after will be destroyed.

All stage combat must be carefully planned and rehearsed. Eye contact must be established, and you and your partner must practice your moves "out of distance," meaning far enough from each other so you cannot possibly make physical contact. If a combat move requires you to make physical contact— pushing or pulling, for example—the victim still controls the action while making it look otherwise.

Armed stage combat (with a weapon, real or fake) is too dangerous to attempt on your own, without a qualified instructor. The unarmed combat moves described here, even though they

*The great Gene Kelly (second from left) and his swashbuckling cohorts in* The Three Musketeers *(1948)*

don't involve weapons of any kind, still need to be done with extreme care. It's essential that only the *character* be surprised by the violent act, never the *actor*.

## Faking a Slap in the Face

An onstage slap is a highly effective dramatic device. The victim is always shocked, and the sharp sound of the slap always surprises the audience. *Whack!* Though it seems relatively simple to deliver or receive a slap, the action happens in several stages. Follow the directions and work slowly and carefully.

Pick a partner, someone whom you trust and who trusts you. Make a solemn oath never to hit or hurt. Don't ever try a contact slap. It's one of the most dangerous forms of stage combat. Your face is delicate and easily injured. A hard slap might break an eardrum, nose, or jaw, or knock out a tooth. A flying finger could poke an eye or deliver a terrible scratch. Then find an adult who can be a spotter (someone who stands close and makes sure things go according to plan).

Next, give yourselves enough room. You don't want to risk falling into a table or chair or slamming into someone. Or, if it's a nice day, find a big patch of lawn. Now you're ready to go to work on the noncontact slap.

You and your partner will alternate playing aggressor and victim, but for now let's say you're the aggressor. You want to set up the slap so the audience sees only the story of the slap, not the technique behind it. So you face downstage, toward the audience, so your slap action will be seen clearly. Your victim should stand at a slight diagonal to you, facing upstage, away from the audience. If the victim stands directly in front of you, his body will obscure too much of the slap. Once you're both in position, you're ready to execute the slap. It

★ **David** *I think stage combat is really fun. I learned that it's the victim who controls the action. If you do a hair pull, you grab the victim's hair and then the victim wiggles around and looks like he or she is in pain.*

★ **Joey** *I did a summer program and I learned how to hold a sword, how to fall so I don't hurt myself, and how to do a fake slap.*

## TRICKY SLAPS

Your slap scenes might not always be set up with the victim facing conveniently upstage. In these cases, you rely completely on the director and/or fight coordinator to tell you exactly what to do.

## SLAPSTICK SLAPS

Just for fun, try doing the slap actions out of sequence. It's a good way to understand the need for coordination and timing. You might even get a great clown routine out of it!

happens in five basic steps: *check distance, eye contact, cue, attack,* and *reaction.*

**1. Check Distance** Stand at least three feet apart with your arms hanging comfortably at your sides. This is called being "out of distance." You want to be far enough apart so there's no risk of accidental hits. Test the distance by taking one step forward with your left foot and waving your left arm back and forth in front of your body. If your waving hand is still at least two to three feet from your partner, you should be fine. Your target is not your partner's face.

**2. Eye Contact** Step back into your original position and make eye contact with your partner. If your partner doesn't make eye contact, do not move. Eye contact is crucial in stage combat. It lets both partners know that the work is about to begin. (If you ever attempt a more advanced slap setup, where you're not looking at each other, you need to be completely certain that you establish ironclad cues so no one gets injured.)

**3. Cue** Maintaining your eye contact, move one hand from your side to the Hello, or "Hi, Mom" position. Like a wave, with an open hand to the audience. The movement to the Hi, Mom is the cue. The timing of the cue sets the tempo for the attack. If you take three counts to move your hand into the Hi,

1.

2–3.

Mom, you must take three counts for the attack. You should move from the cue to the attack with one continuous rhythm: one, two, three; one, two, three; one, two, three—like the oom-pa-pa of a waltz. Don't rush through the Hi, Mom into the attack. And don't freeze in Hi, Mom, then suddenly attack. This awkwardness is a distraction for the audience and breaks the illusion of the slap. It also doesn't allow your partner time to prepare.

**4. Attack** From the open-handed Hi, Mom, you keep your elbows bent and swing your hand, fingertips up to the ceiling, across your body at the level of your partner's cheek. Think of wiping the inside of a curved window. Maintain the tempo of the cue. One, two, three. As you reach the end of the swing, your hand will appear on the other side of your partner's body, completing the aggressor's part of the slap. Remember, you are standing at least three feet apart, so there's no chance your hand will accidentally swat your partner.

**5. Reaction** This is the victim's chance to shine. For every action, there's a reaction, and here the victim's reaction comes in three stages: the sound effect of the slap, the head turn (the expected physical response), and the shout, grimace, or clutching of the cheek that makes the slap believable.

5.

4.

Here's one tried-and-true way to play the reaction: as the aggressor moves into the Hi, Mom, the victim is pressing his elbows against his sides and subtly moving his hands to the front of his body at waist level. This is why he faces away from the audience, to mask his movements. The bottom palm faces up. The top palm faces down, like a clap about to happen. As the aggressor's hand passes in front of the victim's face, the victim brings his bottom hand to his top, making a sharp, slapping sound.

Then, as he would in real life, he turns his head in reaction to the slap. If the slap comes from the aggressor's right hand, he turns his head to his right. If it comes from the left, he turns left. The body part that's attacked is always the part that reacts first. You don't clutch your stomach in pain when you get hit in the head. Next comes the reaction. The shout, grimace, or clutching of the cheek is essential to convince to the audience that the slap has happened, and that it hurts!

It's important that the victim doesn't get carried away and react out of proportion to the attack. Keep the character and the size of the slap in mind. Crashing to the ground with a huge bellowing cry would be ridiculous and out of place if the victim is much bigger than the aggressor and the slap is feeble. Move slowly and carefully.

**Pushing and Pulling** You know how to do these actions for real, but creating the illusion of a push or pull without actually pushing or pulling is a bit more difficult. It's all in the acting: your expression, words, and body language. As with every form of stage combat, the victim is in control. Grab a partner again, and stand facing each other at a slight diagonal so your right shoulders overlap. Unlike the slap, pushing and pulling don't involve sleight of hand, so you can position yourselves as you like in relation to the audience.

If you are the aggressor, doing the pushing, place your right hand gently on your victim's right shoulder. Your cue then comes from your victim, who shrugs his right shoulder forward (you keep your arm and hand relaxed). He then moves it backward as he takes a step backward. This action will straighten your arm and give the illusion of your pushing him. You must coordinate your steps to make these moves convincing. Think of pro wrestlers and the shoving dance that they do.

A pull is basically the same action, done in reverse. Be sure to stand at a slight diagonal to each other, shoulders overlapping. Place your right arm on your victim's right shoulder as you did in the push. Your arm is straight but your hand is relaxed. Don't squeeze! Your victim then cues the pull with a slight shoulder move backward, away from you, then takes a step forward that bends your elbow and creates the illusion of your pulling him. Your facial expressions and body language add credibility to the actions. As you practice, be careful you don't accidentally bump heads.

## Fighting in Style:

★ Grab a partner

★ Clear a space

★ Take turns

★ Don't rush

★ Keep your reactions realistic

**Falling** A fall can be the result of a push or a pull, and you can fall in any direction. The thing about a fall is that you, the victim, are in control the entire time, and create the illusion of falling.

• The first thing you need to be aware of is your breathing; falls, in any direction, are done on the exhale.

• Give yourself plenty of time to complete a fall. Work slowly; when you have the technique down, you can speed up.

• Never break a fall with your hands. It ruins the effect and, more important, can be dangerous.

• Keep your stomach muscles actively working and follow the directions carefully so you won't feel the urge to catch your weight with your hands.

**Meltdown** You may have a role that requires you to faint dead away. The principles are the same as other falls, only you "hit" the ground in a kind of melt, like ice cream turning into a puddle on a hot day.

Try this fall on a count of twenty:

**1.** From a standing position, start bending your knees.

**2.** Then curve your body, tucking your chin toward your chest as you slowly melt to the floor. No sharp edges.

**3.** Watch those knees and elbows.

**4.** Keep your chin tucked as you roll onto one side of your spine (never onto the spine itself) and gently place your head on the floor. Somebody get the smelling salts!

**Back fall** A backward fall is easier than you might think. Let's say you are face-to-face with your aggressor, who has just delivered a serious push. (Not really, of course.)

**1.** Take a big step back with your right or left foot, bending forward at your hips so your abdomen touches the thigh of your front leg.

**2.** As you step and bend, reach your arms and head forward to counterbalance the weight of your seat and hips pulling backward.

**3.** Then you basically sit. But not with a resounding thud; that would hurt and spoil the fall.

**4.** As you get closer to the ground (no hands!), turn your body a bit so you don't bash your tailbone, then roll down onto your side.

**5.** Throughout the fall, keep your chin tucked into your chest. It will look fake at first, but with practice you'll gain speed and smoothness and your fall will be convincing.

The first few times you try this fall, you might want to hold your partner's hands as you lower your body. Your partner's support will help you feel the counterbalance, and you'll be able to achieve it more easily when you do the fall on your own.

**Front fall** Maybe your aggressor pulls you off balance and then lets go. You'd better learn how to do a front fall.

**1.** Take a great big lunging step forward with either leg.

**2.** Bend your torso way forward until your abdomen presses against your front thigh. You should be close to the ground at this point.

**3.** Continue your descent with control so you don't clunk onto your knee.

**4.** When you've lunged as deeply as you can, turn your body slightly so you slide onto the floor on your side. You may use your hands a little bit here, but the control is really in your legs and stomach.

**5.** If your right leg is front, tip your body to the left and reach your arms out along the floor, like you're spreading peanut butter.

**6.** From there, you can stretch out to complete the illusion of impact.

## Faking a Brawl

You're certainly not going to try this one at home, but it's still fun to get a sense of how a brawl is done. Even though the actors are creating the illusion of violence, the fact that a brawl involves several people moving quickly around the stage at the same time means the potential for accidents is high. As with all stage

*This fight scene from* Good Will Hunting *(1997) is a good example of exciting and smoothly executed stage combat.*

combat, every action must be carefully timed and choreographed, and special attention must be paid to safety.

One of the challenges of staging a brawl is figuring out how many people absolutely need to be onstage to create the desired dramatic effect, and then streamlining the movement so that a big story can be told as economically and safely as possible. This is done by blocking out moves (see page 98 on blocking) that best support the characters and the play. You want the audience to see individuals as well as the mass, so each and every altercation has to be crystal clear. Too many bodies fighting without breaks in the rhythm will create a blur, so a good brawl has occasional lulls and changes in dynamics that serve as visual pauses and allow the actors to catch their breath. Once the individual moves have been blocked, the entire stage picture can then be assembled. At this point, more adjustments, for safety as well as dramatic impact, will be made.

*The 1948 version of* The Three Musketeers *is chockful of great fight scenes.*

## CLASSIC SWORDFIGHT SCENES

*Captain Blood (1935)*
*The Adventures of Robin Hood*
  *(best version, 1938)*
*The Mark of Zorro (1940)*
*The Sea Hawk (1940)*
*The Three Musketeers*
  *(1948 and 1973)*
*Scaramouche (1952)*
*The Court Jester (1956)*
*Romeo and Juliet*
  *(best fight version, 1968)*
*The Four Musketeers (1974)*
*The Princess Bride (1987)*

**Swordplay** The art of swordplay is best left in the classroom. The potential for injury is far too great to try it at home, so we'll talk only about the fundamental moves that help make it effective onstage and in the movies. Footwork is key. When one actor takes a step forward, the other takes a step backward, and vice versa. This delicate dance keeps a safe, constant distance between the combatants. The contact is blade to blade, never blade to body. And the strokes, even at a distance, never sweep across the face. Even though a modern sword is no sharper than a butter knife, it can be dangerous. An actor treats the sword as if it were as sharp as a razor.

Of course, in a dynamic fight, the actors don't simply shuffle back and forth in a plodding rhythm, swinging their swords. An effective joust has built-in rhythms, tensions, and changes of tempo and body positions that support the actors' timing and technique and add variety and excitement to the fight.

## Stunts

Many stunts are related to stage-combat techniques like pushing, pulling, and falling. Others are best left to the Jackie Chans of this world. Movie stunts like leaping off mountaintops, riding a motorcycle at the edge of a cliff, falling from jet planes—that guy's not really 30,000 feet in the air, is he?!—fleeing from burning cars and buildings, and jumping out of skyscraper windows require specialized training and, often, more than a few camera tricks. Stage stunts include jumping out of windows, too, only from a much lower altitude—we're talking no higher than three feet—and onto a soft surface like a mattress or thick pad; swinging from chandeliers; and crashing into props.

There are loads of great props that create the impression of damage being done:

• Chairs and tables that "break" when thrown or bashed against a hard surface—or a human being

• Windows that "shatter" when hit by flying objects or bodies

• Doors that "fall" off of their hinges when slammed

• Curtains that "tear" when yanked

If you're really intrigued by stunt work, enroll in a martial arts or stunt class. You won't get to jump out of a plane, but you will learn some impressive moves and develop strength, timing, and control.

*With stunts, the victim's reaction tells a story.*

## GREAT SCREEN STUNTS

*Ben Hur* (1959)

*Blade Runner* (1982)

*Titanic* (1997)

*Gladiator* (2000)

*Mission Impossible II* (2000)

*U571* (2000)

*Beverly Hills Cop* movies

All of the Jackie Chan and James Bond films

*Actor Zhang Zi Yi (center) did all her own stunts in* Crouching Tiger, Hidden Dragon *(2000).*

*Take a look at Keanu Reeves's carefully choreographed feats of derring-do in* The Matrix *(1999).*

# Choreography

Almost every dance performance you ever see will list a choreographer in its program. This is the person responsible for making up the steps. Choreography isn't limited to dancing. Film, theater, and musical productions often use a choreographer, too. Productions that are extremely physical—with lots of running and jumping around and bursting through doorways—might require a bit more coordination than what can be accomplished with blocking. If stage combat—an art form in itself—is involved, the director will call in a choreographer specially trained in fight techniques.

A choreographer has to come up with movement that supports and enhances the story. Every step and **phrase** (several steps that are strung cleverly together) serves a purpose. Though performers in musicals tend to have solid dancing skills, not all actors move comfortably or naturally onstage, so a choreographer who works with actors has to be used to dealing with people who want to move well and follow directions but may not be all that adept or graceful. The steps need to be tailored to the performers' abilities so they don't feel awkward or self-conscious onstage. (You've no doubt heard the expression "two left feet.")

The more time a choreographer has to work with a cast, the better. But sometimes steps need to be created and rehearsed over a relatively short period. A clever choreographer will have a deep understanding of the script, a strong sense of how each character should move (a hyper character will move quickly, for instance), a clear idea of how movement should be incorporated, and an appreciation of the actors' natural movement skills. One approach might be to choreograph steps that look spontaneous and natural, like the sort of impromptu dance your parents might do in a burst of joy around the kitchen. **The goal is to create a unified** *stage picture* (what the audience sees) that tells a story consistently and naturally.

You might have taken dance classes as a young child. If so, you have a "leg up." Lots of kids started with tap, a dance

**David** *If you're a dancer, singer, and actor, you're called a "triple threat."*

**Joey** *I enjoy dancing very much. It's really important. You learn your own body limits and how resilient you are. I sprained my ankle and realized that I have to be more careful with double turns.*

*Choreographer Jerome Robbins gets the Sharks ready to rumble in* West Side Story *(1961).*

form with its own built-in rhythm section. Maybe you took a class in ballet, modern, or jazz for a while. Though you may think you don't remember a thing, you do. Your body has **muscle memory,** which—like its cousin, sense memory—is one of an actor's primary tools.

If you've never studied dance of any sort, give it a try. It's never too late to start. If you love the idea of shuffling off to Buffalo, tap may be for you. Maybe the discipline of a ballet barre appeals. Or you might enjoy the freedom of moving across the floor to a jazz beat. Be sure to ask around to find out who the best teachers are. Once you've decided where to go, enroll in a beginner's class (you won't be alone), and be patient. You may not see or feel results for a while. Your body needs time to adjust to new patterns and your muscles need time to stretch and strengthen.

# Musical Theater

If you love to sing and dance, you may want to try your hand—and body and voice—at musical theater, a form that has a long tradition of making people feel happy. What does it take to be in a musical? Besides the skills you're mastering as an actor, you'll need to work on your singing and dancing, because musicals combine all three disciplines.

There are all kinds of dance steps and styles used in performances. A modern-dance choreographer often creates an entirely original vocabulary—only it's made of steps instead of words. Martha Graham, Paul Taylor, Merce Cunningham, and Twyla Tharp are just a few of the many choreographers who have shaped modern dance, changing the way we think about the body, movement, and music. Ballet choreographers usually work with what's known as a "classical" vocabulary, coming up with new arrangements of steps that have been in use for hundreds of years. George Balanchine, the cofounder of New York City Ballet, reinvented and modernized the ways the body can move within the ballet vocabulary. The young choreographer Savion Glover has introduced an entirely new audience to tap's intricacies through a mix of standard and invented steps. Bob Fosse's snappy moves have hooked Broadway audiences on jazz. (Check out the movies *The Pajama Game* and *My Sister Eileen*.) And ethnic-dance choreographers from Africa, Eastern Europe, Asia, and South America have introduced thousands to the movement and music of cultures around the world.

As for singing, don't panic. You probably already sing in the shower or along with the radio. Even if you don't have a great singing voice, you can take voice lessons to learn important vocal techniques—like how to breathe and move seamlessly from words to song and back again—that will enable you to use what you have for all it's worth.

*Savion Glover redefines tap dancing in* Bring in da Noise, Bring in da Funk, *at the Joseph Papp Theater (1996).*

# A Song and a Dance

**G**otta dance! If you want to have the best possible acting instrument, it's a great idea to enroll in some sort of dance class. You don't have to worry about being able to toss off eleven pirouettes at a clip or hiking your leg up to your ear. Your goal is to get your body accustomed to moving through space, fine-tune your reflexes, and improve your coordination and fitness. As a bonus, you'll get rhythm, you'll get music, and you can add another handy skill to your résumé. Who could ask for anything more?

You've probably heard of *Beauty and the Beast; Grease!; Annie; You're a Good Man, Charlie Brown; Phantom of the Opera; Oliver!; The Sound of Music; Fame; A Chorus Line;* and *The Music Man.* And you've certainly heard of *Cats,* the feline-inspired musical that closed on Broadway in 2000 after an amazing eighteen years and seven thousand performances. That's a lot of happy people. (Touring and satellite companies are still performing the show in other cities around the world.)

Check out your local video store for movie versions of stage musicals. The experience on your TV screen is not the same as it would be at a live production, but you'll get a good sense of how musicals weave stories, dancing, and music and lyrics together. Below is a starter list of titles. Some are from shows that appeared on Broadway many years ago. Others appeared more recently. Guaranteed, you'll be singing along.

- *Aida*
- *Annie*
- *Beauty and the Beast*
- *Brigadoon*
- *Bye Bye Birdie*
- *Calamity Jane*
- *Camelot*
- *Carousel*
- *Cats*
- *A Chorus Line*
- *Crazy for You*
- *Fame*
- *Fiddler on the Roof*
- *Flower Drum Song*
- *A Funny Thing Happened on the Way to the Forum*
- *Grease!*
- *Guys and Dolls*

- *How to Succeed in Business Without Really Trying*
- *Jesus Christ Superstar*
- *Kiss Me, Kate*
- *Mary Poppins*
- *Meet Me in St. Louis*
- *Miss Saigon*
- *The Music Man*
- *My Fair Lady*
- *My Sister Eileen*
- *Oklahoma*
- *Oliver!*
- *The Pajama Game*

- *Phantom of the Opera*
- *The Producers*
- *Rent*
- *Showboat*
- *Singin' in the Rain*
- *The Sound of Music*
- *South Pacific*
- *Stagecoach*
- *State Fair*
- *Titanic*
- *West Side Story*
- *The Wiz*
- *The Wizard of Oz*

**Tap into Tap** (above)
Rent the movie Stormy Weather *(1943).*
*It's packed with the fabulous tapping of Cab Calloway, Bill "Bojangles" Robinson, and the Nicholas Brothers. Don't miss the flying splits on the staircase!*

- *You're a Good Man, Charlie Brown*
- *Ziegfeld Follies* (and anything else with the incomparable dancers Fred Astaire and Gene Kelly)

*Playbill, Inc., is the world's best-known publisher of Broadway show programs.*

⭐ **Joey** *I was in* Beauty and the Beast *on Broadway. I played Chip, the Teacup. I did it for two years and three months—a long time. They had two kids instead of just one in the part. They do that a lot. We would switch on and off. We each did four shows a week.*

# Make a Playbill

Every play needs a playbill, also known as a program. It is handed out to the members of the audience as they enter the theater. Besides giving people something to read before the show begins, the playbill provides all kinds of fascinating information about the play and the people who make it happen.

It can be simple: a single sheet listing the title, author, and each person's role in the production. Or it can be as elaborate as a magazine, with a cover photo or illustration of the production; a summary of the play and introductions to each scene (don't give away too much of the plot); cast headshots and biographies (background information on where the actors are from, where they've been trained, and what they've done previously); brief write-ups of the play's author, director, designers, and key crew members; good-luck messages from friends and family; and ads from businesses in the area.

Experiment with different formats. (Hint: most playbills are small enough to stick inside a jacket pocket.) If you have a computer, try using some clip art or intriguing graphics. If you have a scanner or access to the Web, you might scan or import some photos. Whatever you do, keep your audience's interests in mind. In addition to the all-important basic facts about the production, what else might you want to include?

# Romance

**Fake Kissing** It's inevitable that at some point in your acting career you'll be asked to fake a smooch. Depending on your age and inclinations, the thought of kissing may have great appeal or make you gag. This is where your acting skills have to kick in. There are many kinds of kisses.

- The perfunctory peck on the cheek and its even more perfunctory cousin, the "hello, dahling!" air kiss (no cheek contact whatsoever)
- The cherished, comforting good-night kiss
- The sloppy, wet, hello-to-your-love-interest kiss
- The "I'm falling in love" kiss

You may not know how to do any of these yet, but that's okay. You are an actor, which means you have a character to do these things for you. So pucker up! Shakespeare's *Romeo and Juliet* has loads of kissing, and in the 1926 movie *Don Juan,* actor John Barrymore gives an amazing 127 kisses to leading ladies Mary Astor and Estelle Taylor.

If you are called upon to perform a kiss and you either don't really know how and/or don't really like the person you have to kiss, there are simple techniques to get you through.

- Remember, it's your character, not you, doing the kissing.
- If you are positioned so one of you blocks the other's face from the audience's view, you can pretend you're kissing without actually touching lips.
- If the blocking calls for you to press your lips together with passion, you will act up a storm and do it.

And no matter how you feel about your partner, always, always observe these simple rules:

- Have fresh breath; you don't want a fetid odor to knock out your partner.
- No B.O., you know, body odor; see above.
- Keep your lips pressed together, tightly closed.

You will need to work closely with your partner on kissing. No way around it. The two of you, with help from the director, can find a way to effectively simulate (fake) the emotion. Most likely, you won't be asked to perform romantic

⭐ **Jen** *Remember you're both actors in a scene. Understand the other person knows you're not having real feelings for them. There's nothing exciting about kissing someone onstage. In rehearsals, go right to the kiss. Don't put it off. Get comfortable with it, right off the bat. Everyone gets kind of nervous, so do it, move on, and get back to the scene.*

*John Barrymore puckers up with Mary Astor in* Don Juan *(1926).*

acts that are inappropriate to your age. If you are uncomfortable with what you've been asked to do, speak up. Tell a trusted grown-up if you feel shy about telling the director.

**Hugging** A hug is hard to fake. By definition it is a close embrace, so you'll have to give your scene partner a squeeze of some sort. There's really nothing to learn. You've been giving and getting hugs your whole life. What you need to do is keep your character's personality firmly in mind.

Physical contact of any sort sends a message, so you want to be clear as to what message your character is sending. Hug as he or she would and consider who your character is hugging and why. Is it a big, happy bear hug? A gentle, consoling hug? A good-bye forever hug? A passionate embrace? Each of these conjures up a strong image. Though the basic action is the same—arms circling around a body—when the time comes to do it for real, things like hand placement, how tightly or closely your bodies are positioned, and how you hold yourself create miles of difference in how each is read by the audience.

Do you melt into the other person? Rest your head comfortably on her shoulder? Or do you stand stiffly with your arms at your sides while she hugs you? You will have rehearsed the hugging scene so that both you and the recipient of your affection are prepared and respond in character.

*Marlon Brando and Kim Hunter share a passionate embrace in* A Streetcar Named Desire *(1951).*

# Death and Illness

Death scenes often, though by no means always, come toward the end of a play. Wherever they appear, they are a dramatic climax and must be played with conviction or they come off as awkward, shallow, or utterly ludicrous. Think "death scene" and what comes to mind? One typical scenario is a loudly moaning guy gripping his stomach and staggering around. Finally, he falls to the ground, where he twitches uncontrollably, then dies. It can seem pretty silly in less-than-expert hands. So how do you keep from getting a laugh when you meant to be dramatic?

The brutal truth is that people usually don't die all that quickly. But an excruciatingly long, drawn-out death scene staged in real time (it could take hours to die from a wound in the abdomen) is not going to work in the context of most plays. The audience simply won't hang around, no matter how compellingly you suffer and linger. You have to carefully choose what you show, making sure it communicates the action and that it serves the emotional climate of the scene.

In most cases, the actual moment of death is not as interesting as the dramatic moments leading up to it. If your character receives a mortal wound, how did it happen? Is it the result of a fight or a terrible accident? How will you choreograph the action so the end result—the injury, and ultimately death—is believable? You'll have to use a kind of physical shorthand and find the balance between what would actually happen in real life and the practicality of staging.

Though you've probably (hopefully) never seen someone die from a wound, you've seen it dramatized plenty of times. Next time you watch a play or see a movie with a violent death—could be an action flick, a Western, or a Shakespearean history or tragedy—take a close look to see how the scene is handled. Does the action serve the emotional moment of the scene or do you find yourself rolling your eyes in disbelief?

## Dying Convincingly:

★ Watch how other actors handle it

★ Let your body tell the story

★ Add gory details

★ Keep your character firmly in mind

Shakespeare was a master at setting the scene. In the tragedy *Romeo and Juliet,* the deaths of the star-crossed lovers are the result of tragically poor timing. Unaware—thanks to an undelivered letter—that Juliet has taken a sleeping potion, Romeo thinks she has died and, in his grief, swallows poison. Seconds later she wakes and, seeing him dead, stabs herself in the chest. Whew! So much is happening so quickly and we believe it all. How would you go about bringing this complicated scene to life? (See Time Out for Shakespeare, page 129, and page 133 for a list of movies made from Shakespeare plays.)

If it's a death due to illness or extreme old age, pick out a few key elements that convey your character's physical state:

- appearance—messy hair, pus, blood, closed eyes, etc.
- attitude—angry, sad, resigned; a quiet, shrill, or loud voice
- movements and/or position—moving slowly, painfully; lying down? immobile?

Your character must appear weak and move slowly with obvious effort or pain. Your character must seem aware of life coming to an end. Depending on the story and your character, you must act accepting, sad, or angry about this turn of events. Obviously, you're not going to prepare for the part by allowing yourself to actually waste away. Sometimes set designers hollow out a section of a bed so that the actor's body sinks into the mattress and appears to be wasting away. And you can't make yourself sick or old if you're not. Research! Your believability will come from close observation, imitation, and improvisation.

# chapter five

# Character Building

*Character Journal • Building an Observation Bank •*
*Quirks & Tics • Finding Your Motivation • Sense Memory •*
*Method Acting • Body Language • Faking Tears •*
*Monologues, Dialogues & Ensemble Scenes*

What a character! You've heard that before, no doubt in reference to something you've said or done that the adults in your life found amusing or slightly outrageous. The expression means something else when you're talking about acting. When you create a character onstage or in front of a camera, you bring all of the qualities that make someone unique into focus: how he or she looks, sounds, and moves, his or her motivation.

*Peter Sellers takes on the character of French painter Toulouse-Lautrec in* Revenge of the Pink Panther *(1978).*

**Patrick** I like to develop my own character, one I make up in my own mind, and figure out his surroundings. Is he a teen, does he have a girlfriend, a mom, any siblings?

**Rashad** I recently did a play called Best Friends. I played Nicholas, who's an annoying little brother. He's trying to be cool, like the fifteen-year-old high school kids. I came up with his look: sunglasses and a backward hat.

**Valeria** Everyone says when you're acting to be yourself. But I find that completely wrong. The thing that's most fun about acting is the chance to be someone else—trying out that person, seeing what that person's life would be like.

Once you've determined some basic physical facts—male or female, old or young, large or small, weak or strong—you can begin to think about how to make that person come alive, with a detailed personal history and a particular way of reacting to the world. Let's say your character is a young man. Is he a big tough guy who swaggers and struts? Or is he skinny, jittery, and shy? What does his voice sound like? Deep and gruff? Squeaky, like fingernails on a blackboard? How does he dress? And how old is he, exactly?

One of the great things about creating a character is your chance to transform into somebody else. Remember, you don't necessarily have to like the way your character thinks or behaves. Can you really like someone who's greedy, makes nasty comments, and brags? You just have to be able to empathize, to see the world through his eyes. Here's where all of your careful observations of human behavior come into play. So, go to town!

What else do you know? You've decided age, body type, and the way he moves, talks, and dresses. Now take time to daydream about his inner life. Is he a deep thinker or a guy who does things on impulse? What sorts of books does he read? Or does he stick to magazines? Does he have a hobby? Maybe he's a passionate baker who's happiest elbow deep in bread dough.

Maybe you're portraying a lanky thirteen-year-old girl who has brown eyes and short blond hair, wears leggings, big T-shirts, and platforms, and never seems to sit still for more than ten seconds. Is she generous or selfish, gentle or rough? Does she like pancakes? How does she behave when she's alone? She might twirl her hair and think happy thoughts as she hums to herself. Or maybe she tends to flop on her bed and sulk.

Take time to explore the qualities that make your character unique. Think of everyday frustrations, like being stuck in traffic or waiting in a long line. Does your character curse wildly or remain calm? And what about everyday pleasures like a walk in the park? Does your character pause to smell the roses or race through, oblivious of the fresh air? Now let your imagination run wild. If your character were in the Olympics, which sport? If a flower, animal, machine, or holiday, which one? These playful thoughts will add depth and interest to your character work.

It's a good idea to keep a **Character Journal** so your observations and brilliant ideas aren't lost. A loose-leaf binder is a good idea. It allows you to move stuff around easily as your interests develop (and you can decorate the cover!). You'll soon find you have a valuable **observation bank** that you will refer to again and again. There's no wrong way to structure your journal, though you'll probably want to start with the most basic physical observations, followed by details about body language, dress, behavior, and a list of fanciful "what ifs."

For example, the man you just passed on the street looked uncannily like an ostrich. What was it about him? His birdlike posture? His long-legged stride? Or maybe it was his feathery tufts of hair. Animals are a great resource for character building. Their unusual shapes, movements, and behavior—even the way they use their senses of sight, smell, hearing, and touch—can inspire an actor

**Evynne**  *In character work you have to determine the who, what, where, when, and how so you can approach what you're doing in the best way possible.*

**Joey**  *When I'm working on a character, I look at people on the street and see if the person I'm working on might be like any of them in some way. I keep a notebook with notes about characters I've done in improvs, monologues, and scripts.*

# Goofy Laughs, Rubbery Limbs, and Other Appealing Quirks

**W**hat is it about Cameron Diaz's goofy laugh? Jack Nicholson's jack-o'-lantern smile? Jim Carrey's rubbery limbs and superelastic face? Woody Allen's perpetually anxious expression? (What *isn't* this guy worried about?) These endearing physical traits are a big part of what makes these actors stand out from the crowd, and are as much a part of who they are in real life as in the roles that they play.

*Cameron Diaz,* There's Something About Mary *(1998)*

There's probably someone you know who has an unusual way of walking, talking, or gesturing. Can you imagine how that mannerism would be magnified if seen onstage or onscreen? Would it come across as charming or merely irritating? What about you? Is there something you do that seems oddly

*SCTV's John Candy (left) and Eugene Levy (right)*

appealing? If so, were you aware of it before someone pointed it out to you? Sometimes an actor's mannerisms are so overwhelming that they define his or her entire identity. This can be a disaster, and extremely limiting in terms of roles. Who wants to be typecast as "the guy who always talks like Bugs Bunny"? Eh, what's up, doc? Most of the time, though, actors we like are liberated by their natural quirkiness. Their laugh, walk, expression, or voice adds dimension to their characters and never feels contrived or like a cliché.

working on a character's development. You may want to sup-plement some of your notes with drawings; a simple sketch (feathers and long gangly legs, in the case of your ostrich man) can help you recall certain gestures, an unusual feature or arti-cle of clothing.

# Motivation: Working from the Inside Out and the Outside In

You know that performing a role onstage involves a lot more than simply reciting lines as you move around the stage. You want to convey a strong sense of your character, not only who he or she is but also what he or she is doing and why. You've done your homework and constructed a rich tapestry of experiences that give your character dimension. Let's go back to that thirteen-year-old girl. You know what she looks like and how she carries herself. And you've made several other important decisions. You've created a rich back-ground for her, determining things like where she is from, whether she has siblings, and what her parents do for a living. You also know if she is a happy or sad person.

So how do you go about "becoming" this person? Or do you? There are so many different philosophies, schools, and approaches to creating and building character. All involve close observation and imagination. Some actors talk about approach-ing character work from the "inside out." In this instance, you "represent" the character by tapping into your own emotions and experiences and being attentive to the behavior of others. Others work from the "outside in," "presenting" their characters

⭐ **Marcus** *I like to work on characters who are very different from me. It's more of a test of my abilities.*

⭐ **Jen** *I wouldn't consider myself a method actor, but there are things I definitely use. Sense memory teaches you concentration and helps you picture things in detail. I guess I am more of an advocate for using the imagination.*

*Angela Bassett as Lady Macbeth in* Macbeth, *the Joseph Papp Public Theater, New York Shakespeare Festival (1998)*

to the audience. Your movements, gestures, and voice in the context of the play are what ultimately shape your character, not just your own emotions or experiences. You'll discover that almost all actors use a bit of both.

Take a look at one scene in a play and try to determine what is going on with your character right now, and who, if anyone, is also in the scene. Make it your business to know everything about the time and location. It's smart to do a little background research. If the play is set in the past, learn about how people lived and what was important to them in that time and place. If it takes place in the present, tap into your own memories and experiences for background material.

It's helpful to further your exploration through improvisation. Think of various scenarios that aren't in the play and how your character would behave. Keep at it and your character's particular ways of moving, talking, and reacting will develop naturally. Since you have a mental map of the entire play, you will find it easier to get to the essence of the scene and work on creating a multidimensional character. You can even dress the part. An appropriate, well-chosen item of clothing—a long skirt, a hat, a pair of heavy boots, etc.—can help you get into your character's mind-set.

Imagine this: You're walking down the street, minding your own business, when suddenly, out of the blue, someone throws a bucket of freezing cold water on you. "Arrrggghhhhh!" You shriek, gasp, and sputter. "How dare you!" All of your responses are genuine. **There's not a bit of acting involved.** The passersby who are witnessing your shock and surprise don't need any convincing. In fact, your response is so persuasive that they are shuddering and shivering in empathy. Could you re-create this scene onstage, without the benefit of ice water? Of course you could. You have such a clear memory of the experience that you can call up all of your feelings and reactions simply by remembering the incident.

Another day you are walking down the same street, lost in your thoughts, and you pass someone who is wearing perfume. The sweet smell wafting your way seems familiar and makes you feel happy and secure, but you can't say why. Ah-ha! A few blocks later you realize it reminds you of your grandmother. Or maybe you hear a song on the radio that makes you cry, stirring up memories of a powerful, long-gone summer experience.

With a technique known as **sense memory** you don't need the actual cold water, scent, or song to re-create a convincing response onstage. Developed by the Russian actor and director Konstantin Stanislavsky (see Method Acting, page 78), it involves searching for a physical sensation or memory that will provide an organic and recognizable response to a situation or object that isn't really real. And when you use it onstage, you aren't reliving the emotion as you experienced it. That would be too stressful and distracting. Instead you are using it as a tool to get into the interior life of the character.

★ **Stephanie** *I have to dig into the character and find out what he or she looks like and how they act around people and how they act when they're alone. Are they lonely? Are they hyper? I like to make up my own characters, but if I'm given a character I work with what I'm given. Sometimes I can wear my own clothes. Other times, I change into what I think the character I'm working on might wear.*

★ **Jen** *I love performing and everything. But I also love working on a character, making a name on a sheet of paper into a real person. As you read the script over and over again, you find out new things. Every character becomes a little part of you. When the character is totally different from who you are, you have to find that person within yourself. You get the chance to do things onstage that you wouldn't do in real life.*

# Method Acting

"**I** am not interested in a truth that is without myself; I am interested in the truth that is within myself." These words were written in 1924 by Russian actor and director Konstantin Stanislavsky (1863–1938). A great observer of human nature, Stanislavsky developed a system of relaxation, concentration, and sense and emotional memory exercises that helped actors to empathize with their characters in a truthful and natural way.

This technique, known as the Method, has to do with breaking down stereotypes so actors can get into the interior life and behavior of their characters on a deep level, sometimes going beyond pretending to actually becoming that person.

Stanislavsky believed that by tapping into actual memories, actors could respond to imaginary objects and situations onstage as if they were real, in the process creating a believable performance. Under his direction, actors "inhabited" their characters rather than "presenting" them to the audience

*Robert De Niro goes to physical extremes in* Raging Bull *(1980).*

through melodramatic gestures and artificial speech patterns.

These methods started a revolution in theater that continued to develop in the 1950s, under the direction of Lee Strasberg and his colleagues at the Actor's Theater in New York City. Marlon Brando, Elia Kazan, Stella Adler, Marilyn Monroe, Dustin Hoffman, Joanne Woodward, and Al Pacino are among the best-known Method actors. They actually seem to become their characters. Check out Brando's Stanley Kowalski in *A Streetcar Named Desire* (1951). He *is* that angry guy in the torn, sweaty T-shirt.

There are many wonderful examples of actors whose physical transformations push their performances beyond pretend, all available on video or DVD.

When Robert De Niro played the boxer Jake La Motta in *Raging Bull* (1980), he trained for months so he could fight in peak form, then proceeded to gain an astonishing sixty pounds and "lose" his hair to illustrate the boxer's sad decline. Russell Crowe performed a similar feat in *The Insider* (1999), adding tremendous heft and a balding wig to communicate his character's aging and depression. One year later, he morphed again, appearing as the muscle-bound hero of *Gladiator* (2000). In *Cast Away* (2000), Tom Hanks goes from beefy to scrawny—downsizing fifty pounds and growing copious amounts of hair and beard to illustrate the effects of being stranded for four lonely years on a desert island.

In addition to gaining or losing impressive masses of weight and hair, each actor infused his role with dimension and truth. Even if such extreme changes had not taken place, the level of commitment in their performances makes us believe they have really become their characters.

Actors who practice this technique train themselves to allow the happiness, fear, grief, elation, and frustration that they have encountered in their own lives to come together with the whole experience of being an actor. Because actors are so tuned in to the world around them, they also develop a "sixth sense." Contrary to popular opinion, there is nothing supernatural going on; no ghosts or strange voices. All it really means is a keen intuitive power, an ability to understand and, ideally, to interpret behavior.

Let's say you have to convey a sense of brotherhood with an actor you hardly know. You might even have a brother, but the close relationship the playwright has created for you and your acting brother is not exactly how it is for you and your real-life sibling. Though you and your real-life brother are very close as well, the playwright has added a twist that's not part of your experience: your character has a fiercely competitive streak that creates tremendous friction and adds a layer of tension to your interaction with your onstage brother.

*Alec Baldwin has the title role here in* Macbeth *at the Joseph Papp Public Theater, New York Shakespeare Festival (1998).*

So how do you create believable behavior from this imaginary situation? One way is to recall real-life feelings. "But," you say, "my brother and I never fight." Okay. But certainly there are times when you feel competitive. You wouldn't be human if you didn't. How do you draw on those feelings and apply them to your characterization? Since humans respond to life on an emotional and sensory level—what if you couldn't taste, smell, hear, see, or touch?—relaxation and sense memory exercises are a good start.

To do this kind of work, an actor must be physically relaxed. Relaxation helps your concentration as it enables you to let your emotions out and allows you to let go of concerns and distractions.

# Body Language

**Y**ou are born with an intuitive understanding of body language. The deliberate turning away of a shoulder, the jiggling of a leg, or the clenching of a jaw send unmistakable signals about a person's state of mind. Onstage, body language must become amplified.

**Be Clear!** Every gesture has weight and meaning. And your movements—the way you hold yourself and react—are key ingredients in your characterization. Every move, every position, has to be carefully thought out. Much of this work is done early on, during the first stages of rehearsal, when you are investigating your character. (Stay in touch with your Character Journal, page 73.)

**Be Consistent!** As you create your characterization, you develop various physical traits and habits. The rehearsal process shapes and refines your portrayal, so that by performance time your body language is totally clear. You might be a content, easygoing actor who is playing an anxious, angry character whose movements are stiff and sharp. If that body language is quite different from your own, you will have to work harder to get inside the character so that you can be convincing without exaggerating to the point of absurdity. You want to create a character, not a caricature (a cartoonlike exaggeration of someone's physical characteristics and/or behavior). Your powers of observation enable you to pick out key qualities that subtly define your character's body language.

**Be Loud!** If you are performing on a large stage, you need to think about how to communicate those qualities effectively and make sure that your subtle characterization doesn't seem muted to someone seated way back in Row Z. Maybe there is a gesture you can devise that telegraphs the emotion clearly. It may seem overly theatrical when viewed up close but work extremely well when seen from the audience.

# Sensory Perception

There are many improvisation exercises that can help you understand how to use your sense memory. Try the ones below or make up some of your own. Make it a goal to remember your emotions, physical sensations, and thoughts so that you'll be able to re-create each experience using only an imaginative reality.

**Ice-Cream Cone** Go have an ice-cream cone. Go ahead! Tell your parents it's for your acting work. As you begin to lick the ice cream, pay close attention and ask yourself some questions. How does the cone feel in your hand? Are you gripping it tightly? Does the ice cream make your lips cold? How does it taste? Does the flavor seem to get stronger or weaker as you work your way down to the cone? Is the cone supercrunchy or kind of mushy?

**Write a Letter to a Friend** Pick up a piece of paper and a pen, and as you begin to write, be aware of how the pen feels in your hand and whether your fingers are relaxed or tense. Do you rest your other hand on the paper to hold it steady? Is the paper smooth or textured? Are you sitting up tall or is your head practically touching the table?

**Hot Bath** Run a nice warm bath. Put in bubbles if you like. Ahhhh. Does the water feel a little too hot, a little too cool, or just right? Do you sink into the tub all at once or a bit at a time? Do you let your head get wet? Time to wash. How does the soap feel in your hand? Heavy? Slippery? How does it smell?

*Peter Sellers in* A Shot in the Dark *(1964)*

**Develop a Character:**

★ Nail down the body type

★ Create a personal history

★ Dream up an inner life

★ Create behaviors that ring true

★ Add mannerisms, likes, and dislikes

★ Write it all down

Try to re-create each of these experiences using your sense memories. Do you find that you are recalling details clearly and are able to express the actions and sensations? Would someone watching you understand what you are doing? It will probably take some practice before you train yourself to pay close enough attention. We tend to gloss through a lot of our activities, remembering only bits and pieces. Actors need to learn how to focus and be "in the moment," so that they can recall certain behaviors or emotions when a role demands them.

You might have a part that requires you to perform what are known as **private moments** in public: brushing your teeth, clipping your toenails, examining your face for those annoying breakouts, etc. Could you re-create these activities without becoming self-conscious? It's not easy. Take the time to imagine the room, the toothbrush, the sink, and the mirror. How do you move when you're alone? Draw on these memories, actions, and feelings for your character.

# Emoting: Yelling and Crying and How to Do Them on Cue

Big emotional outbursts and extremes of behavior are extra challenging for an actor. And for an actor's voice. You have to be convincing, performance after performance and take after take, without wearing yourself out. If it's anger you are after, what has provoked it and how do you make it real in performance? You should get into what is happening in the script and how that affects how your character feels. Which events have led to the anger? You might also recall something that has happened in your own life that made you so furious that you screamed and shouted until you were hoarse.

However you go about finding that anger, you also have to find a way to express it, on cue, without damaging your voice. The vocal techniques that you have been practicing—breathing from your diaphragm and relaxing your throat muscles—will allow you to project a very strong voice without strain. (See Projection, page 18.)

If a role requires you to cry, you should examine what has happened in the play to bring your character to the point of tears. How does your character feel? If this isn't enough, you could tap into a sad memory or imagine a scenario where you lose a loved one. These sometimes don't work as effectively or quickly as other, less emotionally taxing techniques. You might try reading a sad novel, playing a sad song, or watching a sad scene in a movie. The goal is to find something that will trigger your tears every time you think of it.

Sometimes it helps to use an object that has special meaning, known as a **personal object.** It might be a piece of jewelry, a toy, a photograph, even a distinctive smell or a sound. It doesn't matter. All that matters is that it evokes powerful feelings. Who gave it to you and when? How does it make you feel when you hold it or look at it? Does it make you think about a particular person or experience? What if you don't have the object in front of you? Can you recall the feelings? Once you find one that is effective, you can think of it rather than the event itself and the tears will flow. If you prefer, stare up at a bright light, then blink hard. This makes many people start to tear.

**David** *If they want streaming tears, they might give you drops. But I usually think about very sad images. What if my dogs never came back or my parents were dead? You have to make it vivid. Like I imagine that I am at the funeral, putting a rose on their coffins. I look up and see the sky is clear. . . . It makes you want to cry.*

Don't get too focused on the tears. They may or may not come. Your goal is to communicate the emotion and the pain. Think about the physical sensations of crying:

- a clenched chest and throat
- a stuffy nose
- a scrunched-up face
- maybe a trembling lower lip

You can use all of these to stimulate—or simulate (fake)—crying. You can also work with your breath: one breath in and three short little breaths out, actions that give you the feeling you get in your face right before you cry. The audience will see the emotion and the pain. It can be more powerful to see someone trying to hold in tears. In real life we usually don't want people to see us cry. If the tears just won't happen, no matter how many sad memories or images you conjure up, the makeup guy will pull out the glycerine drops. These fake tears pool and dribble just like the ones you've been known to create yourself.

# Going It Alone (Monologues)

Now that you've warmed up and sampled some character work, have another go at the monologue you tackled at the beginning of *Break a Leg!* You'll find that you have a lot more information under your belt. You know how to prepare your body and voice and have an understanding of various approaches you might take to build and convey your character. This time, try it out in front of a friendly audience: a parent, a supportive sibling, friends. This will give you an opportunity to test your powers of memorization and to work on your performance.

**1.** Ask for feedback. If you get "That was wonderful, dear!" ask for specific comments about your projection and characterization.

**2.** Did your audience feel that you created a believable, multidimensional character? If not, think about what you could do differently.

**3.** Ask your audience about whether you handled the funny material as well as you did the serious, or vice versa.

**4.** Imagine delivering this same monologue in front of strangers next time and how that might affect your delivery, and your nerves. Many actors find it less stressful to perform in front of people they don't know.

It's a good idea to learn a few monologues very, very well, since you may walk into an audition and be asked if you have one that you would like to perform. If you can, pick one that is funny, to show that you can handle comedy, and one that is more serious, perhaps something from a classic play. Try to choose monologues that run between one and three minutes. The idea is to demonstrate—as efficiently as possible—your acting range and ability to perform. In addition to working on the samples in the Appendix, you can find hundreds more in books that are devoted to monologues for young people.

In addition, you should read the entire play before learning the monologue. This way you'll know the story and have the necessary background to complete your characterization. You'll know why your character says and does what is in the scene, and you'll have strong ideas about how to make it all real. You'll also have opinions about how you want your character to move. (See Blocking, page 98.)

**Joey** *Monologues are really important because for a lot of auditions you need to have one. They can be done different ways. If you're doing one from Shakespeare, you make your gestures really big. But I did one from* You're a Good Man, Charlie Brown, *where the kid is really shy, so I made my gestures small.*

**Dialogue:** a conversation between two characters

# Teamwork

**Dialogues** As fun as monologues are, most of your time onstage is spent in **dialogue** with other actors, which is also fun. You have them several times every day, so you are familiar with the back-and-forth that makes them lively. A dialogue can be mundane, about everyday sorts of things, like doing the laundry or getting ready for school. It can be packed with intrigue and emotion. And, like a monologue, it can fill the audience in on action offstage, in the background, and provide insight into a character's thoughts and activities. Unlike a monologue, the use of two actors allows for characters to develop in relation to each other. The audience gets to see the relationship between the two characters as well as learn more about each individual character by watching him or her interact with another. The effect of the dialogue all depends on what the playwright has written and the style in which it's performed. A director, for example, may interpret what seems to be a fairly low-key exchange as something

incredibly fiery (see The Director's Role, page 107).

Your first step is to choose a dialogue. (Look at books that are devoted to dialogues and scenes or start with one of the samples in the Appendix. You might even find an interesting one in a favorite play.) As with monologues, you need to read the entire script first if possible. This gives you a firm grasp of the story and the characters' roles in the development of the theme.

Next step: find a partner. Ideally, this person is also an actor interested in working on a dialogue. If there is no such person available, you can recruit a friend or family member. If this is the case, be sure to explain your goals and instruct them as to how you wish to read. Before you start working on the dialogue itself, talk it over with your partner. Make sure you are in agreement about what the scene is about. You will want to improvise a bit to get a sense of each other's approach to the words and the movement. (See Chapter 3.)

When you begin to work on the actual scene, you'll find that the rhythm of your dialogue—when and how you say

**David**  *If I had to choose, I would choose a dialogue over a monologue because I like to interact.*

**Molly**  *Always look at your partner when you are speaking, and pronounce your lines clearly.*

**Joey**  *Dialogues help with monologues and scenes. You and your partner have to figure out what came before and what comes after.*

**Jen**  *I like a two-person scene better than monologues. In a true monologue, you're only talking to God or the audience or to someone onstage who's not responding. Scenes are so helpful because you can respond to what is being said.*

**Joey** *It's helpful to watch everyone when you work in an ensemble. You can learn from what they do.*

**Jen** *Acting is something I've always been interested in. When I was younger, I wanted to be an actress, singer, or model. I acted for the first time when I was in eighth grade.*

your lines—and how you block (see Blocking, page 98) the scene are as important as the lines themselves. Here are some guidelines:

**1.** The two of you want to shape the words and movement so that the energy of the scene builds instead of remaining flat or petering out. Be conscious of how you and your partner use your body language and voices, and how you fill the space with your actions.

**2.** Be careful not to jump on your partner's line or wait too long before speaking. A dramatic pause is dramatic only if it makes sense to your character and the script.

**3.** Your blocking and the pace of the scene should reflect the intent of the playwright.

**4.** Is it an anxious conversation between two nervous people? If so, your speech will be hurried and may be breathy and high in your throat. Your movements will echo that tension. A relaxed conversation between two close friends requires an entirely different approach. How can your breathing help?

**5.** Run through the scene several times. Look at the script to quickly memorize a line, then look up at your partner while reciting it. Don't say your line while looking at the script. This method will help you memorize your lines and make the scene come to life. Soon you'll be saying your lines and doing the blocking without glancing at your script.

**6.** Try not to prompt your partner by mouthing his or her lines or saying them under your breath. You can't do this in performance, so don't do it in rehearsal! (See You Must Remember This!, page 106, for more about memorization.)

**7.** As you rehearse and rehearse—practice makes almost perfect—the scene will begin to fall into place. You've not only memorized your lines and your partner's, you're finding new ways to enhance your character and give the scene vitality.

Soon you'll want to perform the dialogue before an audience. Even if it's just Mom, her presence and support will make it feel like an event.

# Ensemble Scenes

There are many instances when you will be in a scene with several actors at the same time. Your concentration and focus need to be extra sharp because there are so many words being said and so much activity going on. And you need to **cultivate a healthy sense of give-and-take.** When you are part of an ensemble you are sharing the stage, and therefore the spotlight. The rhythm of an ensemble scene is almost always going to be more complex than that of a monologue or a dialogue. Think of an ensemble scene as a chamber orchestra and each actor as an instrument.

How does your instrument (character) fit into the mix? Again, you need to have an overview of the entire script to be an effective participant. If you aren't clear about your character's intent or actions, no one else will be, either.

As always, improvisation is a great tool when it comes to creating a bond between the actors, getting at the essence of a scene, and establishing that all-important rhythm.

**1.** Figure out how your character interacts with the others, and your role within the larger structure of the scene.

**2.** You want to stay open-minded to the other actors' interpretations. If you approach an ensemble scene with a rigid idea of your character, you'll never get past doing something that feels false and stiff.

**3.** Make an effort to coordinate your movements with those of the ensemble. If you are off on a tangent all your own, your characterization will be disjointed and distracting.

Once you start working on the scene itself, you'll be comfortable enough in your role to begin memorizing your lines and blocking. Stay involved in the process of realizing the ensemble's action, but don't interfere. Don't take on the role of director. This will create roadblocks in your character development and resentment among your fellow thespians!

# chapter six

# Reading Between the Lines

**Analyzing & Marking a Script • Tragedies & Comedies • Avant-garde Theater • Rehearsals • Blocking • Entrances & Exits • Finding Your Mark • Memorizing Lines • Stage Fright • Direction • Etiquette • Roles • Casting**

I f someone recommends a great novel to you, don't you want to read the entire book from beginning to end? If you were to read just the two middle chapters, you would be cheating yourself. You wouldn't know what happened before or after. Or if you skipped way ahead to the very last few pages, you'd know the ending but you wouldn't care much because you would know nothing at all about how the author got there. You'd be in the dark about the story and the characters.

*Like actors everywhere, these two performers at the Guthrie Theater in Minneapolis, Minnesota, spend quality time with their scripts.*

The same logic applies to reading and analyzing a script. Even though you are most likely playing just one role, you need to know the entire story and become familiar with all the parts as well as the playwright's style in order to make intelligent and meaningful decisions about how to create your character.

# Reading and Analyzing a Script

It's important to read through the script on your own several times to get a clear idea of what the playwright is trying to communicate. The first read-through gives you the big picture: the story and a sense of who is who. The second and third times, you develop a keen understanding of the play's structure and of how the playwright uses language to convey action and feelings. You also start to form strong feelings about how you might approach your role and how your character relates to the others. Your ideas about these relationships will probably change as you read and begin to rehearse.

*A typical first read-through*

**theme:** sometimes also referred to as the **spine,** it is the main idea or ideas that run through the script

You want to consider the playwright's goals, and whether he or she has introduced a **theme** that revolves around the characters' lives or one that is larger than the play itself: the environment, the importance of family, or the trials of being a teenager, for example. The script may be thought-provoking, funny, or sad. Or all of the above. Then there is subtext, the real meaning behind what a character says. Also referred to as "reading between the lines," it's a way of getting at the truth behind the words. If a friend says to you, "There was this guy sitting next to me at lunch who chewed with his mouth open. It was gross," he or she might really be saying, "Hey, [your name here], close your mouth. I don't want to watch you mash your food."

Most scripts tell a story with a definite shape, or *arc*. The pieces are as follows (in order):

**1. Setting the scene** establishes the location and time of the play, where and when the story takes place (also known as the **context** for the action).

**2. The buildup,** or **conflict,** which is the development of the story and twists and turns of the action.

**3. The climax,** which is the turning point in the story, often but not always at the midpoint of the play.

**4. The resolution,** which is how the conflict is resolved after the climax; how everything works out and finally comes to a conclusion.

Once you determine the arc of the story, you can begin to work on your character's journey within it. (See Marking a Script, page 105.)

# Structure of a Typical Performance

A typical performance divides the play into the acts and scenes that are indicated by the playwright in the script. These acts and the scenes within them are designed to tell a story and keep the drama moving forward in the most effective way. Not every scene is action-oriented with a beginning, a middle, and a neat resolution. Some are created as transitions, zooming in on a particular event that gets actors from

**Joey** *First I read the script over, then I usually try to figure out what could be happening in the scene before and after. For each line you figure out the character's objective and how he should sound. I make notes about all this in the margins.*

**Jen** *With any script you have to read it many, many times. You have to know the play. I underline the things other people in the play say about my character. I work on finding what I call my character's center. Picture your character, walk around, and write down your ideas. You've got to have a journal. I write stream of consciousness, filling in all the stuff that's not in the script. I also collect things, like something in a magazine, or a postcard, and tape it in my journal.*

point A to point C, or to reveal aspects of plot or character. For instance, the playwright of a murder mystery might have scenes showing various characters doing suspicious things in order to confuse the audience about who the murderer is.

There are often, but by no means always, two acts separated by an intermission. This is a short period of time (usually fifteen to twenty minutes) during which people in the audience stretch their legs and maybe buy a snack, sets are changed, technical glitches are fixed, and actors grab a few quiet moments to catch their breath and change or touch up their hair, makeup, and costumes.

**An act is a chunk of action** that contains from one to several scenes. Act 1 of *Romeo and Juliet,* for example, has five scenes. As indicated by Shakespeare, scene 1 takes place in "Verona. A public place," scene 2 in "A street," scene 3 in "A room in Capulet's house," scene 4 in "A street," and scene 5 in "A hall in Capulet's house." This action-packed act is followed by four more acts and nineteen more scenes!

A change of scene can represent a change in location, a different time of day, or something more symbolic, like a dream or a memory. If the curtain doesn't come down, or close, how do you know that the scene has changed? A director may choose a dramatic device like a "blackout." The lights go out for a moment, and when they come up again the scene has changed. There may be a new set in place or just a sense, because of the blackout, that it's a later or earlier time. Other effective ways of changing scenes are to lower and raise painted background drops and introduce or remove set elements in front of the audience's eyes by using pulleys or stagehands. (See Chapter 8 for much more on what goes on behind the scenes.)

# I Laughed! I Cried!

There are, of course, many types of scripts: tragedies, melodramas, dramas, histories, comedies, satires, musicals, and experimental, to name a handful. Some are sad. Some are funny. Some are sad and funny. And some are filled with fantastic events that can happen only in the realm of the imagination. Most scripts contain elements of a few types. You're probably familiar with some of these categories from television, the movies, and the many books you've read. A serious drama, just like a serious event that has happened to you, might very well include moments that are funny or silly. This contrast keeps things interesting, and more like real life.

Tragedies are among the oldest forms, dating way back to ancient Greece. (We're talking 500 B.C.E.) They are always serious and usually feature a hero who goes through some sort of emotionally wrenching, life-changing experience. Examples: Shakespeare's *Romeo and Juliet* and *Hamlet* and Martin McDonagh's *The Lonesome West* and *The Beauty Queen of Leenane,* which are contemporary plays about life in Ireland.

Comedies include scripts that make you chuckle or laugh out loud as well as those that simply end happily. Examples: Molière's *The Bourgeois Gentleman* and *The Imaginary Invalid,* seventeenth-century satirical comedies that make serious fun of that society's customs, and David Ives's *All in the Timing* and *Lives of the Saints,* modern one-acts filled with witty banter and satire.

Experimental scripts, sometimes referred to as "theater of the absurd," deal with situations that are imaginary or an intricate mix of fantasy and reality that might comment on the absurdity of life. Examples: Samuel Beckett's classic *Waiting for Godot* and contemporary playwright José Rivera's *Maricela de la Luz,* about a girl who rescues her brother and parents from a magical otherworld filled with spirits.

"Groundlings" watching a performance in Henry V *(1945).*

# Avant-garde Theater: What Is It?

**E**xperimental is also known as avant-garde, a French term that translates as "foreguard" and is used to describe art that is unconventional and ahead of its time. Avant-garde work aims to change the status quo, to shake things up. Sometimes it comments on things happening in politics or society. The term could apply to a play, a movie, a painting, a dance, a building, or a piece of music. Often, something is called avant-garde when it is influenced by art from different, seemingly unrelated disciplines. For example, a dance might shift rapidly from one movement quality to another, a characteristic that you associate with the quick cuts of film. Or a play might contain lots of carefully composed stage pictures, reminiscent of a painting or sculpture. Emotions and events may be expressed in surprising ways. An actor may cry out, then start laughing hysterically for no obvious reason. Or lie down in the middle of the stage and appear to go to sleep. Taboos are broken in an effort to forge new artistic territory and disrupt old patterns.

In the case of theater, the fourth wall—that imaginary barrier between the performers and their audience—may be demolished, allowing the viewers to become part of the action. And the action they are part of is filled with new ways of thinking and seeing. There are more questions than answers. There are no explanations. What it all means is up for grabs. Each member of the audience fills in the blanks with his or her own ideas.

A few fun shows that make every effort to smash the fourth wall are *Mummenschanz*, Blue Man Group's *Tubes*, and *Stomp*.

*Blue Man Group shatters the fourth wall.*

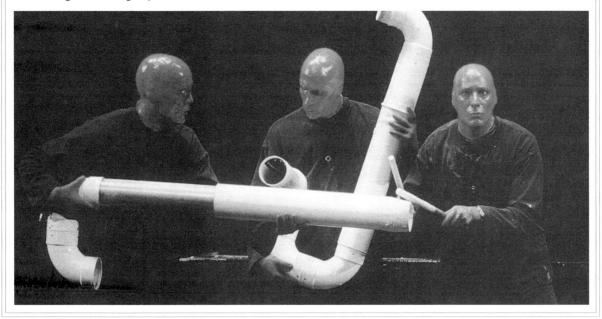

# Rehearsal

Though each director has his or her own way of working, the rehearsal period almost always begins with the entire cast assembled around a table, in a rehearsal studio, or on the stage to read the full script out loud. This is called the **first reading** or **read-through** (see photo below). It can be nerve-wracking. Each actor is trying to read his or her part well and, at the same time, impress the director and get a sense of the other performers. Who are these people and what do they think of me? A good way to work through a first reading is to make eye contact with your fellow actors. You'll feel like you're not alone, and you'll begin the process of establishing rapport.

Once you've gotten through the first reading, the director might give you his or her personal take on the play and how it will be realized. You might get instructions about how you should deliver your lines and begin to learn some **blocking**. Depending on the director's way of working, you may have an opportunity to experiment with your characterization. By all means, do. At this point you'll still be reading from your script,

**Joey** *I've done some script readings. They're a really good experience. You're surrounded by all these great people, and you get to try out a new show. And that's really cool.*

**Patrick** *It's good to get everything down pat. But if you mess up, don't show it.*

**David** *You read the character description and see how he responds to situations that he's put into. You have to put yourself there, and try to listen to what other people are saying. If you listen to other people's lines, you will get where you are coming from. If you are supposed to say, "Sally ate all of my candy," you need to know which of those words to emphasize so what you say is in context. If you say, "SALLY ate all of my candy," it means something different from "Sally ate ALL of my candy."*

## WHY REHEARSE?

Because if you don't rehearse, you won't know what you're supposed to say or when and where to say it! And because if you don't rehearse, the audience—the people who are spending time and, often, money to sit and watch the performance that you are part of—will see something slapdash that is awkward and often painful to watch. If they don't bolt at the first intermission, they will let you know what they think during the curtain calls.

Depending on the size and budget of a production, the rehearsal period can range from a couple of weeks to several months. However long, it is a time to master your lines and blocking and experiment with various aspects of your characterization: your voice, the rhythms of your speech, and your movements and gestures.

but you'll be making marks on it (see Marking a Script, page 105) and starting to think about memorizing lines, emotions you'll need to convey, sense memory you'll need to call on, and more.

**Looking and Listening** Soon you will be expected to know your lines and blocking. At this next stage you will start to explore your characterization more fully (you're not carrying around the script, for one thing). It's crucial to keep your eyes and ears open to the director's instructions and comments and pay attention to how your fellow cast members are beginning to shape their roles. You will find that certain things you try work wonderfully while others seem awkward or out of character. **Don't be shy about exploring.** That old expression "Nothing ventured, nothing gained" applies to the rehearsal period. Your instincts, along with the director's feedback and instructions, will guide you.

**Blocking** Unless the performance calls for you to sit on a stool or at a table and read from a script, your character will need to move around the stage in relation to the other actors and to the set. The director gives these movements, known as **blocking,** to you, and along with your lines they form the scaffold for your character's actions.

Think about how you move through your daily routines. It's breakfast time and you are hungry. You open the refrigerator and grab

*Actors learn their blocking in rehearsal.*

the juice and maybe a yogurt or the butter for your toast. Where's the toaster? Oh, yes, you need a glass. So you go to the cupboard. While you're there, you take a plate. Then you reach into the drawer below for a butter knife or a spoon. All of these actions happen in patterns. You do them every day, so you're probably not all that aware of which paths you take to get from here to there—like how you detour around the counter to get to the fridge or which hip you use to slam the drawer shut.

But on a stage, it's most important that you move in a conscious way. For one thing, you need to avoid crashing into the set elements. If they can't be in place for rehearsals, their locations and **footprints,** the space a set piece occupies on the stage, should be clearly marked on the floor with masking tape. If there is supposed to be a table in the middle of the stage, you'll want to know to walk around it, not smack into it.

You also need to understand the reasons why and how your character is moving. This is called **motivation.** Your hunger for breakfast motivates your rapid movements around the kitchen. If the director tells you to walk quickly to the **downstage** right corner when another character enters from **upstage** left, you need to know why. (See Which Way Is Up?, page 100, for more on stage directions.) The motivation behind the actions is key.

A character who is sad about having to visit a sick relative might move slowly and lethargically. Later in the scene, he or she may learn his or her loved one will make a miraculous recovery and suddenly become ecstatic. This new state of mind might be expressed through large, bouncy movement with lots of devil-may-care flinging of limbs. If you don't take

**Melanie** *I like to rehearse because I like to do my scenes in front of people, but sometimes I get shy.*

**Evynne** *Acting isn't about dressing up in costume. It's about learning the techniques and discovering who you are.*

**Joey** *During rehearsal, stay focused, keep your professionalism, and stay happy. If you're uncomfortable, you should say so.*

**David** *One of the best things about acting is the feeling of accomplishment. After weeks or months of rehearsal, you know you did it and the audience likes you. When my friends see the show, they say, "Wow!"*

**David** When you are doing
blocking, you always want to have
a pencil and write down everything
that the director tells you. If you're
supposed to put your hand on your
head and tap your foot at the
same time, you better write that
down. If the director tells you not to
do something you're prone to do,
like folding your hands, you write
that down. When you're memorizing your lines, you practice your
blocking.

the time to figure out the reasons behind each movement, your actions will look robotic or purposeless. Play with dif-ferent motivations for the blocking and see which ones work best for your character.

**Which Way Is Up?** For this demonstration it's easiest to work with a **proscenium** (pro-SCENE-i-um) stage in mind. In a proscenium theater, the type that you'll encounter most often, the audience watches the performance through a "proscenium arch," a large opening in the wall that separates the stage from the **house,** or auditorium. This opening is also known as **the fourth wall,** an imaginary wall that separates the performers from the audience (see page 96).

If you are lucky enough to have a real proscenium stage handy, great. If not, it's relatively easy to create one. Find a room with a fairly large empty space. You can always shove furniture out of the way. If it's a square or rectangular shape, it will be easy to visualize the different areas. If it's circular, create a square or rectangle inside the circle. You can use fur-niture, shoes, lengths of string, anything that enables you to define the edges.

Just as a map has directions that describe whether you're located north, south, east, or west, a stage can be divided into sections that indicate where you are in relation to the audi-ence: upstage, downstage, center stage, left stage, and right stage. Why up and down? These terms are left over from the days when stages were built at a slant ("raked" is the technical term) to improve the view for the audience. The back of the stage was higher than the front. The performers literally walked uphill to get to the back of the stage **(upstage)** and downhill to get to the front **(downstage)**. Newer theaters rake the auditorium's seats rather than the stage, which gives everyone in the audience an unobstructed view of the stage and eliminates (most of the time, anyway) the need to peer around elaborate hairdos or hats.

Using the diagram below as a reference, make a mental map of your stage. Once you've decided where you want your audience, it's easy to figure out what's up and what's down. You know that if you locate north on a map all the other directions fall into place: east is always to the right of north and west is always to the left. It's a no-brainer to find south. Time for a tour. Hint: downstage, the portion of your stage that's closest to your audience, is your stage's north.

Stand in the center of your downstage and face the audience. You are standing "downstage center." Take several big steps backward and you're officially "center stage." Make a three-quarter turn to your right and walk on a diagonal to

| UPSTAGE RIGHT | UPSTAGE CENTER | UPSTAGE LEFT |
|---|---|---|
| CENTERSTAGE RIGHT | CENTERSTAGE | CENTERSTAGE LEFT |
| DOWNSTAGE RIGHT | DOWNSTAGE CENTER | DOWNSTAGE LEFT |
| **AUDIENCE** | | |

your stage's upper right corner and you'll be in the territory known as "upstage right." Hey, but which way are you facing? Not only does the stage have a map; your body has its own positions within it. This does not mean that you're in two places at once.

Confused? Take a moment to do a bit more tromping around, and it will become crystal clear. Come back to center stage and turn your back to the audience. You are standing center stage and facing upstage, also called **full back.** Make a half turn to face them, and you're still standing center stage but facing downstage **(full front)**. Now make a quarter turn to your right **(quarter right)** and walk forward on a diagonal to downstage right and make a quarter turn to face stage left. Where are you and which way are you facing? (Downstage right and **profile left.**) Try out several of your own moves. Kind of like being a chess piece on a giant board, isn't it?

**Marks and How to Find Yours** When you are performing, you can't look down to see if you have hit your "mark," the exact spot where you are supposed to be at a given moment. This would be breaking character. Your mark might be a particular piece of furniture or a spot on the stage itself indicated by tape. One good way to be sure you get

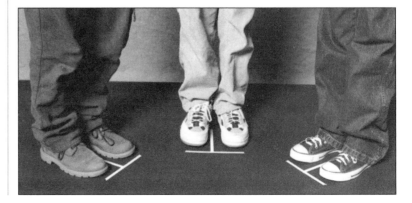

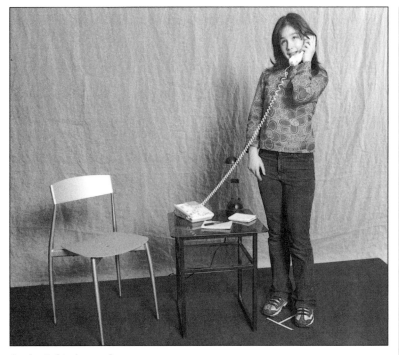

*Stephanie hits her mark.*

where you need to be during a performance is to practice by standing on your mark and saying the line that is supposed to get you there while walking backward to your earlier position. Use this technique only when you have a short distance without any obstacles you might trip over!

For example, let's say your line is "Lucas, did you know that Aunt Sophie keeps piranhas in her backyard?" In the script you are supposed to start saying the line at your kitchen sink and complete it just as you reach your refrigerator, walking at a casual pace. Try it out, starting at your refrigerator and walking backward to the sink. You might get there too early or too late. Be sure to rehearse your blocking at performance pace. Try this several times, then say it again walking forward. You will soon find that you are able to hit your mark without having to check. This simple technique can be applied to screen as well as stage acting.

**Jen** *When a director gives you blocking, you can't just say, "Okay." You have to justify the action. Are you getting a glass of water from the table because you're thirsty? Know why you do everything, or you won't be comfortable in performance.*

## GREAT COMINGS AND GOINGS CAPTURED ON FILM

### Entrances

- *Gone with the Wind* (1939): Rhett Butler (Clark Gable) makes his first, and very dramatic, appearance at the foot of the grand staircase, setting the tone for his roguish character.
- *Cleopatra* (1963): A victorious Queen Cleopatra (Elizabeth Taylor) cruises into Rome via the Tiber River, dressed as the goddess Aphrodite.
- *Ace Ventura, Pet Detective* (1994): Ace (Jim Carrey) bursts into a ballroom, ridiculously disheveled and soaking wet after battling a shark in the bathtub. "Whatever you do, don't go in there!"

### Exits

- *The Wizard of Oz* (1939): Dorothy (Judy Garland) makes a glamorous departure from Oz with a click of her ruby-shod heels.
- *Mission Impossible II* (2000): Ethan Hunt (Tom Cruise) pulls off a hair-raising parachute exit from a skyscraper.
- *O Brother, Where Art Thou?* (2000): Ulysses Everett McGill (George Clooney) makes a hilariously swift exit from a moving train, yanked by the chains that link him to his fellow cons—who are still on solid ground.

## Entrances and Exits

A big part of blocking involves working on how your character enters and exits a scene. Entrances provide strong clues to physical health, age, and personality, as well as to state of mind:

an angry entrance will look and feel different from one that's grand or devil-may-care. A character's first entrance is especially important. Like the impression you get of someone you meet for the first time, it comes with a wealth of information. You prepare for each entrance by getting into character before you set one foot onstage or in front of the camera. **Get your face, body, and voice into the act;** though you can't speak out loud if you're standing in the wings, you can vocalize softly. If you wait until you're already in sight, you'll confuse the audience and your character will lose credibility.

Exits are equally significant. How your character leaves a room—your walk, your posture, whether you're silent or singing—speaks volumes to whoever is left in the scene. Depending on what has just happened and where you are heading, the other characters may feel a sense of loss, relief, or complete indifference. The same goes for your character and his or her impact on the audience. And when you exit, **don't drop out of character until you're out of sight;** even though you might not be

able to see the audience as you saunter offstage, they certainly see you. You'll destroy the illusion if they catch sight of you giggling or swigging a bottle of water.

**Marking a Script** You build a role from a combination of what's written in the script, your understanding and interpretation of your character, your reactions to the other characters and events in the story, and the instructions and guidance of the director. The more you know about the script and your role within it, the easier and more rewarding the process will be.

An important part of building a role involves marking your script with detailed notations about the story, setting, and characters—yours in particular—and about the way you'll deliver your lines. Think of it as a kind of diary of your role.

**1.** Get yourself a workbook with blank paper. A three-ring binder is ideal. Just be sure it is small enough to balance in one hand when open. You'll be carrying it around when you start to rehearse your role.

**2.** Make a copy of your script.

**3.** Tape it onto the blank pages in the binder, trimming the edges of the script so that it is surrounded by a border of plain paper where you can jot down notes about the play and your character.

**4.** Leave several blank pages at the back for more general notes. You will get some from the director about the overall style and mood of the play, the design of the costumes and set, etc.

**5.** Highlight your own lines in one color and your stage directions in another. The script will contain directions from the playwright about the scene and your character's actions as well as the director's instructions, which you'll

## Analyzing a Script:

★ Get an overview of the story

★ Determine the mood

★ Find the theme

★ Establish the rhythm

★ Construct your character

*A marked script reflects an actor's insights.*

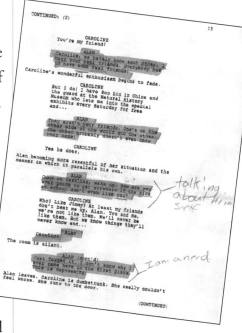

CONTINUED:

She does not afford him an answer. Alan shifts uncomfortably.

ALAN
I was actually waiting for someone.

CAROLINE
Who? I'm the last one on the route.

Alan is stumped. He leans toward the window and buries his face in his book. Caroline leans over until she is practically on top of him. She is trying to see the title of his book. Alan's eyes appear over the cover. He is disturbed.

ALAN (cont'd)
What?

CAROLINE (cont'd)
(an excited yelp)
CRIME AND PUNISHMENT?

ALAN
Shh.

Alan is mortified that someone might have heard. He scans the aisle but no one is looking.

CAROLINE
You're reading Dostoevsky! I love Dostoevsky! That's such a great book especially the part with the axe!

She imitates chopping and then continues, her words practically tripping over eachother.

CAROLINE (cont'd)
Whack! Uhhh! But you know what's really the greatest is White Nights! You have to have read White Nights! Have you read White Nights?

ALAN
No. I don't like love stories.

The bus stops. Alan quickly rises to exit. Caroline continues as she follows him.

CAROLINE
Oh, the snow! It's so romantic! The wintertime! Russia!

*Oh, is she making a pass at me?*

(CONTINUED)

write in the margins, about entrances, exits, and blocking: *Get up quickly, throw off your shawl, and run to the window.*

**6.** Write your own observations about your character's motivations, actions, gestures, mannerisms, and tone of voice in pencil since they may very well change as you continue to work on and develop your role.

**7.** You want to make this character you are bringing to life as three-dimensional as possible. His or her posture and movements must reflect state of mind as well as the events of a particular scene. Your character's speech patterns are also important. Be sure to indicate different tones of voice: stress, pitch, rhythm, volume, and quality (see Putting Your Voice to Work, page 16). You may also want to insert marks that indicate where, for example, you take a big breath and pick up or slow down the tempo of your speech.

**8.** In addition to moving around and speaking, your character makes and responds to all sorts of sounds. There are the verbal sounds we all make that aren't words per se, but carry loads of meaning: sighing, grunting, sniffing, tongue clicking, laughing, throat clearing. And there are the nonverbal sounds that lend atmosphere and indicate mood and state of mind: shuffling papers, tapping feet, snapping or drumming of fingers, slamming doors. Mark down everything!

**9.** Don't forget to include your ideas about what your character is thinking: this subtext provides crucial insight.

# You Must Remember This!

How do you memorize lines? Putting the script under your pillow won't work. Neither will cramming right before a rehearsal. Start by reading the script, then reread it.

# The Director's Role

**T**he director is the one person responsible for how all of the artistic elements of a production come together: the lighting, costumes, scenery, sound, and of course the acting. He or she must have a thorough understanding of the script and strong ideas of how to interpret it so that it comes alive.

Among the many things a director considers are:
1. What the script suggests in terms of style and setting.
2. How many and who the characters are: their genders, ages, and circumstances.
3. How many scenes there are and the special requirements of each.

A director is there to guide and support the actors, to help them find the motivations and rewards of their characters. The more experience a director has had in real life as well as in the theater, the more he or she can bring to this task. Knowledge and appreciation of how people behave are just as useful as knowing the difference between upstage and downstage. Just like teachers you've had in school,

some directors are easier to get along with than others. This is a fact of life. A good director will create a positive atmosphere that makes the actors feel secure as they explore and begin to define their roles.

You've probably noticed the director scribbling in a notebook during rehearsals. It's not a letter or a grocery list. The director is keeping careful track of everything from a missed line to mistakes in blocking to a new thought about the rhythm of a particular scene and, at the end of every rehearsal, will give notes (sometimes called footnotes) to the cast. When you get a note, listen carefully. You will be expected to incorporate the requested adjustments or changes in time for the next rehearsal. If a note is not clear, ask questions. If, after an expla-

nation, you are still unsure or don't agree with the note, try to find a time to speak with the director in private. Though a good director will be encouraging and supportive and listen to your questions and ideas, it's important to remember that he or she has the final say.

If you encounter a director who has a short temper—there is no excuse for yelling—gives fuzzy directions, or seems unreceptive to your efforts in rehearsal, you might try talking to him or her in private, but only if you feel comfortable doing so. If you feel shy or intimidated, you should speak to someone who has authority over the director.

*James Cameron directs Leonardo DiCaprio and Kate Winslet in* Titanic *(1997).*

**ad-lib:** to improvise a line or speech on the spot. You'll need to do this if you or a fellow actor forgets a line.

Make sure you grasp the plot and your character's role in the action, what he or she wants and why. The more you understand your character's intentions, the more sense your lines will make and the easier it will be to memorize them. Also, if you happen to forget a line (it happens), you'll be able to **ad-lib** a convincing response. The words will come easily. Don't act, react.

Some actors learn their lines before actual rehearsals begin. Others wait to learn them along with the blocking. If you choose to learn your lines ahead of time, you will be able to concentrate on developing other aspects of your role in rehearsal: how your character walks and gestures, how he or she interacts with others. Just be sure that you don't get too attached to your private approach. Once you're in rehearsal with the director and the rest of the cast, you may find that your character needs to evolve in new ways.

There are several ways to memorize your lines:

**1.** Use a tape recorder. Record every scene that you're in, reading all of the parts aloud. Record your character's lines in a softer voice than those of the other characters. Listen to the scene several times, a little at a time. Recite your lines softly along with the tape. When you feel like you're beginning to remember them, speak in a voice that's louder than your voice on the tape. If you start to forget, say them softly again so that the recording can prompt you.

**2.** Read through your lines, memorizing them bit by bit. Read a line. Read it again. Now cover it and recite it a few times. Did you get it right? Uncover it to check. Go through the entire scene this way several times. When you feel that you have the scene down, move on to the next one. Maybe you and a partner can work on the script together. Your partner will prompt you by reading the lines that come before your lines, over and over again. Each of these processes will help you to memorize your cue lines as well. *When* you say your lines is as important as *what* you say.

**3.** Learn your lines along with your blocking. As discussed above, this will help you by associating your lines with specific movements as you develop your character and respond to the other actors. Some actors find this method the easiest because their lines are never isolated from their performance. In either case, you will want to spend quality time with the script before rehearsals begin so that you are confident of your understanding of the story and the characters.

# Stage Fright

You know the feeling. It could be butterflies in your stomach, cold, clammy palms, a superdry mouth, shaking hands, a pounding heart, or all of the above. You might even get weak in the knees and feel as if your mind has gone blank. What's going on? Call it nerves, performance anxiety, or stage fright—almost everyone who gets up in front of an audience experiences a few of these symptoms in one form or another.

Whether mild or severe, they are the result of adrenaline, a chemical your body releases when you get excited, nervous, or scared. It's perfectly normal to feel a bit keyed up or

**Jen** I used to have more trouble memorizing lines, but your memory is like a muscle. I'm pretty quick now. Basically it's a matter of going line by line, repeating each one until you know it, then going on to the next.

**Joey** You have to know your lines. Learn them and the ones before and after. You need to be organized. And you need to learn the right techniques, like how to project your voice.

**Patrick** I usually tape my lines and listen to them at night on headphones. I think about them when I'm sleeping, then in the morning I know them.

**Jen** *I've never had that much stage fright. I might get a little nervous in the wings. I take a breath. Once I get my first line out, I'm fine for the rest of the show, even if I have to exit and enter.*

**David** *Sometimes I get butterflies and sweat a lot. I go over my lines and exercise my voice. When I step onstage I say my line and there's a pulsing in my stomach and I don't realize I'm saying my line, but it's all natural. Practicing gives you an automatic reflex. In the middle of the scene your confidence returns.*

*Stage fright can happen to anyone. Check out Piper Perabo's character in* Coyote Ugly *(2000).*

anxious when you perform. In fact, it's a healthy reflection of your desire to do well. Your goal is to learn how to turn whichever symptoms you experience into tools that help you focus and concentrate. The following information, tricks, and tips are useful for any kind of public speaking—from a birthday toast at a family gathering to a school presentation in front of your class.

First, remind yourself that you are very well prepared, and that your audience is not your enemy. Those people sitting out there are on your side and want you to do well, whether they're your classmates, a director at an audition, or a theater full of paying customers. Though you may imagine your shaking hands or quivering voice are all your audience is seeing and hearing, it's likely they aren't noticing anything unusual if you're focusing on your performance rather than on your fears. Remember: you are not having an out-of-body experience!

With these good thoughts spurring you onward, you can learn how to use your nervousness to help tune up your body and mind for the demands of performance. There are several simple techniques you might try. Keep in mind that no two people are the same, and part of your process as an actor is discovering which methods work best for you. If one doesn't seem to do the trick, try another.

**Breathe** Breathing is essential to relaxation and concentration. Review the Find Your Diaphragm exercise on page 10. Concentrate on the calming air moving in, and the tension moving out. When you breathe deeply from your diaphragm, you won't hyperventilate (shallow, rapid breathing that can make you quite dizzy), your voice won't sound like fingernails scraping against a chalkboard, and you will relax enough to be aware of where you are and what you're doing.

**Voice It** You may find that in addition to deep breathing, you'll want to do some face and voice exercises (see Chapters 1 and 2) to chase away excess tension and keep you from becoming cotton-mouthed or tongue-tied—not happy states for an actor. Pay attention to your articulation, which can get muddy or rushed when you're nervous. If your mouth feels like a desert, try sucking on a lemon or taking a whiff of vinegar (backstage!) to get your saliva flowing.

**Work It Out** Many actors find that physical exertion calms their bodies and nerves and helps them focus. They might prepare for a performance by going for a jog or a swim, taking a dance or yoga class, or running through a series of body warm-ups (see Chapter 1). You want to feel relaxed and alert, so don't exercise to the point of exhaustion. You don't want to fall asleep in the middle of your monologue!

**Relax and Refocus** Some actors prefer to keep their bodies quiet and find their concentration by turning their focus inward rather than directing their energy out. Many find it useful to focus on peaceful imagery as they perform gentle breathing exercises. Imagine you've been transported to a tranquil and beautiful setting. Maybe you're stretched out on powdery white sand, gazing at turquoise waves. Or you're on top of a snowcapped mountain looking down into a green valley. Whatever works.

**Patrick** *When I have stage fright I feel myself getting very red and I start to shake and sweat. I have to overcome that fear. I take a deep breath and close my eyes and say, Oh please, let me do good.*

**Valeria** *I used to have stage fright, but I've gotten more comfortable. I don't look at the crowd. And I don't make faces if I do something wrong. Usually people won't know if you've made a mistake. So I just keep going.*

**Stephanie** *When I have stage fright, it's not a big fright. I get a little nervous at the beginning, but then once I'm onstage I feel relief. I've accomplished so much to get there.*

> **Jen** Tech rehearsals are so long. No one likes them. Dress rehearsals are a chance to make sure things are working, like whether or not your costume feels right. If you've been rehearsing in jeans and suddenly are wearing a big pouffy skirt, some things you've been doing with blocking won't work.

> **Joey** Dress rehearsals really help because even though there is no audience, you're doing a performance and you have a chance to figure out stuff that goes wrong.

**Dedication and Focus** Some actors overcome stage fright by dedicating their performance to someone they love or admire, directing their energy to that connection and away from their fears. Others look to the audience for reassurance. They might focus on a particularly friendly face or imagine that the entire audience is a gathering of close relatives who think they're perfectly wonderful, no matter what they do or say. What could be more comforting than that?

There is no right or wrong way to cope with stage fright. Experiment and try to remain open-minded. Some techniques will work better than others. It may be that a combination of several techniques is your key to achieving calm. The goal is to feel in control and enjoy being "in the moment."

# Tech and Dress Rehearsals

It's getting close to opening night. You know your lines and blocking backward and forward, and nearly everyone else's, for that matter. You are confident about your work and about how your character fits into the play as a whole. It's finally time for the technical (**tech**) and **dress** rehearsals, when lighting, sound, costumes, props, and scenery start to come together. It can be a hectic period. Cues can go awry, a prop can get misplaced, a costume can be too tight or too loose. Whatever you can think of, it can happen.

Despite the long hours and seeming chaos surrounding you, you need to keep your cool and your concentration. Tech rehearsals are always long; this is the chance for the crew to get every technical detail just right. Yes, you're nervous and excited. And it seems like things will never be finished in time for the opening. But they will be. Use this time to fine-tune your performance and **become accustomed to all of the other elements** that complete the show. Does that wig fit, or will it topple off of your head when you bend forward to take your bow?

Sometimes a director or producer will invite friends and colleagues to watch the dress rehearsals. Their presence will give you an idea of what it's like to perform in front of an audience.

# Various Roles and What They Mean

There's a saying that there are no small parts, only small players. What this means is that even if you have only one line—a famous one-liner is "Dinner is served"—you say it with as much passion and commitment as if it were just one line among hundreds. In other words, no matter what size part you are given, perform your lines (or line, as the case may be) with energy and presence. An actor who looks down on a part because it is small will give a "small" performance and, in the process, become a "small" player.

So let's say you audition for a play and are offered what's known as a **walk-on** (a part that involves one entrance—that's why it's called a walk-on—and usually just a line or two). You might be playing the role of a butler at a fancy dinner party, and when it's time for the guests to be seated you enter the drawing

*Jake Lloyd*

## CASTING CALL

Director George Lucas's casting call went out for an eight-year-old to play Anakin Skywalker in *Star Wars Episode I: The Phantom Menace.* But that didn't stop the agent of then-six-year-old actor Jake Lloyd (see photo above) from sending in a photo. As luck would have it, several years went by before the part was finally cast. Though by this time he was ten and had an impressive amount of acting experience under his belt—two feature films and several TV shows and commercials—Jake was small enough to pass for eight. So he was cast as the slave boy who wins his freedom to start training as a Jedi knight. And because his face had changed so much over the years, he was not yet known to a wide audience. He was free of baggage.

Once again, however, Jake is too young. In *Episode II* his character is now a teenager falling in love with a full-grown Natalie Portman's Queen Amidala.

## ETIQUETTE

It's easy to get so caught up in the process of rehearsing and performing and so jangled by nerves that you forget your manners. Not a good thing. If you are rude, even unconsciously, to the director, your fellow performers, or the crew, it will reflect badly on your work. Be considerate: dress appropriately, be on time, pay attention, refrain from distracting conversation, and recite *your* lines only; no one appreciates an echo. And don't chew gum.

Never interrupt the director or anyone who "has the floor." You'll gain respect and probably learn something while you're waiting your turn. When you do speak, keep your comments positive or at least neutral. You don't want to poison the atmosphere with snide remarks. Try hard to keep your complaints to yourself. If there is something really wrong, of course speak up. Always, always, say please and thank you. Your parents *are* correct about this simple rule.

room and announce (drumroll, please!) "Dinner is served," then promptly exit the scene and the stage. Since that's your one and only moment, how do you play it? You don't storm onto the stage and shout, "DINNER IS SERVED!"—unless the director has told you to. And you don't throw the line away by muttering inaudibly or swallowing your words—**DINNER** IS served—unless the director has told you to. You play that line fully and in character. Keep in mind that directors pay close attention to how an actor behaves in rehearsal. If you have a bad attitude toward your work, it will be noticed and have a negative effect on the rest of the cast and on your own performance as well as any future parts.

A **cameo** is similar to a walk-on, but may involve a bit more time onstage and is often performed by a well-known

actor whose appearance might be a surprise to the audience. You've no doubt seen movies where this has happened. You may be offered a **supporting role.** This is just what it sounds like: a role that supports the main player or players. Think of a friend who helps you complete a school project or a younger sibling who's always orbiting around you, getting in your hair. It might be a fairly large part, depending on the play. Most plays have several supporting players, which makes perfect sense when you remember that there are rarely more than one or two stars in a single production.

Maybe you've landed the **starring** role. Wow! It's a huge responsibility. You will be onstage a lot (start learning those lines!) and your character will be the focus of much of the action. Most starring roles are played by actors with lots of experience, though there are occasions when a **novice** (someone brand new to the theater) is chosen. If the unknown is a girl or young woman, she's often referred to as an **ingenue.**

In many instances, an unknown actor demonstrates the particular qualities the director and producers are looking for. It could be that he or she fits the part physically and appears to have the talent and discipline to master the role. Or it could be because of a certain innocence, energy, or charm. You never know—that someone could be you.

# Understudies

Let's say you audition for a role and the director asks you to be an understudy. An under *what?* An understudy is an actor who is hired to learn another actor's part in case the other actor cannot perform for some reason. This is nothing to sneer at. Though you weren't the director's first choice for

**Molly** *You can't get carried away and talk backstage or the people onstage will be drowned out by your voice. Once, during a performance at the Lee Strasberg Studio, someone was talking backstage when my best friend was performing. Her part got drowned out. Directors and agents come to see these plays and try to hook you up with people. No one picked her up because no one could hear her. It was bad.*

**Joey** *Don't bother other cast members. Some of them get upset and aren't too patient.*

**Jen** *The really good actors are always a little bit early. They're walking around, doing vocal warm-ups. Also, be "off book" as soon as possible. Memorize your lines. And be respectful of the director, even if you disagree.*

A **novice** or **ingenue** is an actor who is a clean slate, an unknown, free of the baggage carted around by a celebrity known for certain types of roles.

★ **David** *Being an understudy is a drag sometimes because you have to be there every night and most of the time you don't get to go onstage. But you might get to go on, and you get to meet lots of people. It's another opportunity to be in a show. I understudied a role on Broadway and one of the kids got fired, so I assumed the regular role.*

the role, there was something about you that seemed right. Right enough anyway for the director to choose you as a potential stand-in.

As an understudy you will attend rehearsals and learn all of the lines and blocking as if you were going to perform the part yourself. But since you can't very well follow the actor you are studying under around the studio or stage like a shadow, how will you actually rehearse the role? You will have to work on the part somewhat in the background: off to a side of the studio, in the wings, wherever you can watch what's happening and hear the director's instructions. You may or may not have a chance to work onstage. Most likely you will have to grab moments here or there—before, after, or during a break in rehearsals—to try out your blocking and get a sense of the set.

So what happens if you are called into action? The actor you are understudying has come down with a terrible cold and can hardly speak. Chances are, there won't be much, if any, time to prepare. This is why you have been rehearsing so diligently on your own. If you are lucky, and if there is enough time, the director will arrange a quick run-through. Most of the cast will be supportive—some of them have been in your shoes—but some may be impatient and not pleased about having an extra rehearsal. Try not to be distracted. Though you will be nervous and anxious about how you are doing, make every effort to stay calm and think of it as an opportunity. This could be your big break! More than one understudy has gone on to stardom. The director, not to mention the audience, will get to see you perform. And if you do really well, the next time you're up for a part it may be yours.

# chapter seven

# Pulling It All Together

**The Greenroom** • **Gaffes** • **Hamming & Upstaging** • **Curtain Calls** •
**Encores** • **Flops** • **Ovations** • **Shakespeare** • **Slang**

The big moment has arrived! You are excited, prepared, and
eager. You have worked out all of the kinks in your part, and
asked the director for extra guidance if you needed it.
Your wig finally fits, and you have practiced putting
on your makeup so
many times that you
feel like you could
do it in your sleep.
It's time to put all of
your hard work into
practice in front of a
live audience.

⭐ **David** *When you're in your dressing room, close the door. Don't run around in the halls. Before the curtain, when you're in the wings, be very quiet. Be respectful of your fellow actors.*

*Go over your lines, make sure you know your blocking and everything there is to know about your character. You should know your part in your sleep. Don't get too serious about your work. It's supposed to be fun. Stay relaxed.*

# Opening Night

Stage fright, bungled lines, technical snafus, and unpredictable behavior from fellow actors can all affect whether the magical transition from rehearsal to opening night is silky smooth, bumpy, or somewhere in between. While there's no magic spell to ward off potential mishaps, your own state of readiness will help you make the best of whatever comes your way.

The stage manager or the director has given you an official **call.** (See What Does It Mean to Call a Show?, page 140.) This is the time, similar to curfew, that you are to be in the theater before the performance. It will be an hour and a half to two hours ahead of **curtain time,** the time that the show begins. Don't be late. Your professionalism is on the line. When you

arrive, you will stash your belongings in the dressing room, do your body and voice warm-ups, and get into costume and makeup. Some actors prefer to get dressed and made up and then do their warm-ups. You'll discover through experience which routine works best for you. If you're sharing a dressing table, be considerate of your neighbors and keep your area neat.

As it gets close to curtain time, the stage manager will start giving warnings: half hour, fifteen minutes, and five minutes. You need to pay attention to these announcements so that you can be sure you're ready to go when he or she calls **places.** You then take your place backstage to prepare for your first entrance or go to what's known as the **greenroom** to wait until it's time for your entrance.

You're on! Concentration and focus are key, as always, and will help you turn the nervous energy and excitement of opening night into positive performance energy. Even if you don't feel especially nervous, you can be sure that some members of the cast do. Be sure to tell everyone, including the stagehands, to "Break a leg!" (Read more about superstitions in Legends and Lore, page 120.)

Keep in mind, along with everything else you've jammed into your brain, that the audience is on your side. Everyone sitting on the other side of the curtain has made the effort to be there and wants to enjoy the experience of live theater. This means that they will forgive and probably forget mistakes. You should, too. They will be fixed next time around. The show must go on!

*Opposite: The crowd goes wild in*
Shakespeare in Love *(1998).*

★ **Jen** *The second show of every performance is awful. It's like a curse. Opening night, there's adrenaline. The second night, energy drops. Then the third night is awesome again.*

★ **David** *Balancing time between your acting, social life, and school life is hard. When I was in Abby's Song on Broadway, I was tutored on the set and fell a little bit behind. My school was great about it and I caught up. It was worth it in the end, to know I'd done a good job and worked hard.*

# The Run

You got through opening night with flying colors. Bravo! Now you have the luxury of "running" the play without that particular pressure. You can make small adjustments in timing, as long as you don't change your lines or blocking (except with the director's okay). You'll find that as you and the other actors become more comfortable in your roles, the play will feel more unified and develop its own flow. But you will never stop working on your performance. Each and every time you step onstage you will recommit your energy and imagination and make new discoveries.

Your approaches to your performance and to the audience are key. Work to maintain the role that you created so carefully during rehearsal. And look forward to the audience's involvement. If you do, the audience will support your efforts by believing in your performance. An actor who "breaks" or "steps out of" character by giving away the story through inappropriate gestures or expressions destroys the delicate balance between performance and reality. Your goal is to present a fully realized character that you are in control of and, most important, that you can enjoy sharing with your audience.

# Legends and Lore

The first time you hear a fellow actor cheerfully call out "Break a leg!" as you're about to set foot onstage, you'll no doubt be surprised—and maybe a little offended. Don't be. Your well-meaning colleague is taking part in a rich theatrical tradition, and wishing you a good performance. This particular expression came about because it's considered bad luck to wish someone good luck directly—you might be giving that luck away—so you do the right thing but in a roundabout manner.

Some actors ensure their own good fortune, hiding talismans inside their costumes (Helen Hayes supposedly tucked a four-leaf clover inside her left shoe) or carrying out personal rituals like touching an ear before stepping onstage, stroking a rabbit's foot, or even picking up rusty nails backstage. Others travel with mascots—tiny figurines, photographs, coins, fragments of cloth—with which they adorn their dressing rooms, where, by the way, whistling is forbidden. (This particular rule has its roots in Elizabethan theater, when sailors were hired to man the backstage rigging and communicated through elaborate whistles. A wayward whistle might get you accidentally clobbered by a sandbag.) The great John Barrymore and his siblings gave one another red apples for luck. These edible charms could not be eaten or their spell would be broken.

Sometimes it's the play itself that is cursed—like Shakespeare's *Macbeth,* a play so steeped in disaster that some actors refuse to mention it by name. At its first performance, in 1606, the boy performing the role of Lady Macbeth (in those days, girls and women were banned from the stage) either got very sick or died. No one knows for sure. Anyway, Shakespeare himself took over, a heroic move that apparently so appalled King James I that the play was kept out of circulation for the next half century. Once it was revived, the misfortune continued. In 1849, the Astor Place Riot took place in New York. Warring fans of the two actors playing Macbeth on the same night interrupted performances and eventually caused a riot that left twenty-two dead and more

century, when stages were lit not by electric lights but by comparatively dim candles and oil lamps. Others say it comes from London's Red Lion, a theater built in 1567, just before the famous Globe Theatre was built (see page 133). The Red Lion had a room called a "tiring house," later known as the "Scene" or greenroom. It was a place where the performers dressed, waited to be called onstage, and sometimes rested. No one knows if this room was *truly* green or if the fact that it rhymes with "scene" somehow resulted in it being called green. Far-fetched?

Still others wonder if the name is connected to the required clothing color (green!) worn after 1572 by members of acting troupes on occasions when the nobility attended. In eighteenth-century London, green came to be associated with the theater: green curtains, green carpet rolled out for heroic death scenes, stagehands in green jackets. . . . Whatever the real reasons and no matter the actual color, we still, for tradition's sake, call the room green!

## Pitfalls:

★ Goofing up an entrance or exit

★ Knocking over a prop or scenery

★ Upstaging fellow actors

★ Flubbing a line

★ Breaking character

**Joey** *In* Beauty and the Beast, *there's a line when Chip sees Belle for the first time and he's supposed to say, "Mama, Mama, you're never going to believe what I saw. She's got two arms and two legs." One time I said, "Mama, Mama, you're never going to believe what I saw. She's got six arms and six legs." I think everyone in the audience noticed. But I just kept going. When you mess up you can't stop.*

than thirty injured. There's more: a 1934 production at England's Old Vic saw four Macbeths in just one week. One actor lost his voice, another caught a cold, and the third was fired. The fourth managed to survive. Orson Welles's 1935 production, a.k.a. "Voodoo Macbeth," featured Haitian musicians who sacrificed goats—in the theater!—before opening night, in an attempt to ward off evil that may have caused the untimely death of the only critic who didn't like the show. Speaking of Shakespeare, the library at the University of Pennsylvania displays a pair of gloves he supposedly wore. But don't dare slip them on. Legend has it that you'll be dead within months!

And then there are the ghosts. . . .

# Recovering from Gaffes and Mistakes

Excuse me, did you just say, "Pass the bullfrog, please?" Your fellow actors—not to mention the horrified playwright, if he/she is watching, the director, and the rest of the backstage crew—were expecting "Pass the butter, please." You can't hit the rewind button and go back in time. Theater is live, happening as you blow your line! And since you're onstage, in front of an audience that's hanging on your every word, it's unwise to stop the play, drop out of character, and say, "Excuse me, folks, I meant to say, 'Pass the butter,' but somehow butter came out as bullfrog." Nor should you laugh or cry—though you may feel like it. You need to maintain the illusion of the performance. If it's broken by a mistake or loss of concentration, the glare of reality sets in and the audience loses belief in the world you're trying to create onstage.

Fortunately, all is not lost. Flubbed or skipped lines, missed cues, and other onstage mishaps are all part of the acting landscape. The trick is to keep your eyes and ears open. "Look and listen" should be every actor's mantra. If you are properly tuned in to what is going on around you and in touch with your character's behavior, there's always a way to get back on track.

Your fellow actors' responses might cue you to a most appropriate way to proceed. If they laugh at your preposterous blooper, you might laugh yourself and get the line out as your character would in real life. "Okay, okay, I know there's no bullfrog on the table, so just pass me the butter, would ya, please?" Or one of them might modify his or her lines accordingly. "Hey, I don't see any bullfrog. How about the butter?" If you forget or skip over a chunk of dialogue, your quick-thinking scene partner might fill in the blanks with a bit of improvised dialogue.

Sometimes a prop gets misplaced or isn't there at all. Let's say your character is supposed to walk to the upstage wall and make a phone call. But there's no phone hanging on the wall. The stage manager—or whoever is responsible for the production's props—has by mistake put it way downstage, on a table next to the couch. How do you react? Certainly not by panicking and shrieking into the wings, "Where is the phone? It's supposed to be right here, on the wall. I can't finish this scene!"

Keep in mind that objects get moved around in real life, too. React in character. Maybe glance around the set and say, "Oh yes, I forgot I moved the phone, now where did I put it?" Once you've found it, go to it, and proceed with the

**David**  In Abby's Song *I was backstage and had to be the voice of an angel. They gave me a mike that would project my voice all over the house. I didn't have the script and was looking at the monitor, watching the star. Then all of a sudden my mind went blank. The soundman looked at me like, "Oh no!" Everyone is hearing me say, "AHHHH." I'm panicking. Then, as soon as the star is about to say her next line to help me, I remembered my line and everything was okay. I made sure not to forget next time.*

**Joey**  In Beauty and the Beast, *there's a scene when Chip the Teacup hugs his mother, Mrs. Potts. One night, when the kid I alternated the role with was performing, their wigs got tangled and they couldn't move. Chip says, "Do I have to still sleep in the cupboard, Mama?" and instead of just laughing and the two of them running offstage, she said, "Oh no, sweetie, we'll always be together," and then they hobbled off.*

scene as rehearsed. If a prop isn't there at all—this also happens—you may have to put your improv skills to use. Try not to get flustered. Whatever you do to keep a scene moving in the right direction, do it as your character and the audience will be convinced.

# Curtain Calls

When it's all over, the curtain closes—or if there's no curtain the lights go out—the audience starts to applaud, and you scramble to your place for the **curtain call.** Also known as *taking bows,* the curtain call is a traditional way for the audience to thank the actors for their *wonderful* performance, and for the actors to acknowledge and thank the people in the audience for their *rapt* attention.

Your director may choreograph elaborate curtain calls that present members of the cast in character and in order of importance. Remember, there are no "small" roles. Or the entire cast may be instructed simply to walk onstage and

**curtain call:** the curtain is opened, or lifted and lowered, depending on how it's hung; the performers bow; the curtain closes

form a single line and bow as "themselves." Actors are very sensitive to where they are placed in curtain calls, so most directors take special care when designing them.

Curtain calls usually correspond in feeling to the mood of the production itself. If it's a comedy, the bows might be playful. If it's a tragedy, they will probably be solemn. There are infinite variations on this tradition.

# Ovations and Encores

If you're lucky enough to have attended a performance that got a **standing ovation,** you know what a thrill it must be for the performers. The people in the audience are so excited and involved that they don't want to go home until they've shown their appreciation by standing, clapping, and cheering. The performers gladly come out for bow after bow, and the curtain can open and close many, many times before the audience gets tired and finally goes home. The world record goes to opera star Luciano Pavarotti for a 1988 performance

# Playing to the Crowd vs. Hamming It Up

Egos are a good thing. But sometimes they can get out of hand. Actors need to be assertive and proud of their work, but never at the expense of being aware of and generous to their colleagues.

You know what a ham is. Not the kind you eat, but the kind who hogs the spotlight whenever there's an audience. "Hey, everyone, look at me, aren't I the greatest?" Your translation: loudest, rudest, most obnoxious (a.k.a. an ego-maniac). You probably have had more than a few hams in your classes at school. You may even have one in your family. As long as a ham's performance is restricted to goofing around on the playground or at the dinner table, it's harmless and can be ignored. But it can't be ignored when it happens onstage. Hamming it up onstage under-mines the play and the other actors' performances.

There's a big difference between using the stage as a handy excuse to show off and playing to your audi-ence—performing in a way that respects and serves the material. Actors sometimes ham it up, also known as mugging or overacting, because they are self-conscious, nervous, or compensating for being under-rehearsed. If they realized what they were doing, they would be embarrassed.

One way to avoid switching into "ham" gear just because there's an audience is to stay in touch with the discoveries and techniques of the rehearsal pro-cess. Ideally, the rehearsal period has helped establish rapport and a spirit of collaboration among the cast, so that every-one involved feels supported, confident, and part of the whole. If hamming or upstaging (grab-bing inappropriate attention from your fellow performers by doing something manipulative) happens in rehearsal, the direc-tor should stop it immediately before it becomes a habit in performance.

Even if just one person in a cast of twenty mugs, the spell of the play will be broken. The production will be about the actor demanding the disruptive attention, and the audience, as well as anyone who has to share the stage, will quickly become exasperated and irritated.

in Berlin. The great singer received 165 curtain calls and a sixty-seven-minute standing ovation. Do you think he was just a bit worn out?

Sometimes, after several curtain calls, performers will bow in front of a closed curtain. This brings them much closer to the audience, practically to the edge of the stage, and is the most intimate kind of curtain call. It also gives the stagehands a break from hauling the ropes that open and close the curtain. Often, especially in dance and music concerts, the ovation is so enthusiastic that it results in an **encore,** which means the repetition of a work already performed or the performance of a special piece designed to come after an ovation. This can lead to another ovation, more curtain calls, another encore, and on and on.

# Flops

It's sad but too true that occasionally a production will totally flop. It might be the quality of the writing, the story, or the acting. It could be a combination of all three. Whatever the reasons are, the audience doesn't respond or, more likely, responds negatively, with just a smattering of applause and maybe even some booing. Not a happy situation for anyone involved. Sometimes the critics—the people who write reviews for newspapers, magazines, television, and the Web— love a play but it flops with the audience. For some reason, the public doesn't connect with it, tickets aren't sold, and it has to close soon after it has opened. Sometimes the opposite happens, and audiences fall in love with a production that all the critics seem to hate. This is a happier situation because tickets are sold and the production stays open for a long time.

**Joey** *I know a kid who was in a show called* Whistle Down the Wind, *in Washington, D.C. It closed after a few months, and never made it to Broadway. He was so upset because it was his first big part. But he got into another Broadway show.*

The best scenario, of course, is when both audience and critics agree that a production is wonderful and not to be missed. Tickets are sold, there are great reviews, so more people hear about it and even more tickets are sold. Everyone is happy. Imagine being part of *The Fantasticks,* the world's longest-running musical, which celebrated its fortieth anniversary and 16,562nd performance (!) on May 3, 2000. It is still playing at the Sullivan Street Playhouse in New York City's Greenwich Village, the same 135-seat theater where it opened. Talk about staying power! But you don't have to be a New Yorker to see it. There have been over twelve thousand productions in America, and more than seven hundred in at least sixty-seven other countries around the world.

**Not every show can be a hit,** obviously. Most actors have experienced an undeniable flop at one time or another. If it happens to you, you will, understandably, be upset and probably even angry. You've worked hard, after all, and had high hopes for a success. Your fellow cast members and the crew may have felt they had a hit on their hands, only to find out they didn't.

**Try not to take it personally.** Try instead to learn from the situation. Focus on the good work you did to prepare for the show. Think about what you have learned about your craft, about the new acting skills and insights you have developed that will help you in the future, and about how you have grown as an actor. Your ability to deal positively with disappointment is as important a skill as learning how to handle great success. Being able to put things into perspective will serve you well, no matter what you do. And remember, there will be lots of other opportunities. *Your* show will go on.

# Time Out for Shakespeare

Everyone loves a great story, packed with intrigue, romance, and adventure. William Shakespeare, born in Stratford-upon-Avon, England, in 1564, was a master storyteller. Apparently never at a loss for wonderful words, Shakespeare, a.k.a. the Bard (which means poet or storyteller), was the incredibly industrious author of thirty-seven plays and a slew of gorgeous poems and sonnets, an output that makes him an all-time storytelling champion. And what stories he tells! He had a remarkable ability to zero in on emotions and relationships. He understood what makes people tick. Whether plumbing the depths of human behavior or exalting in the glories of love, Shakespeare's words, written some four hundred years ago, never grow stale or lose their significance.

But many of those words, and the intricate ways he put them together, are hard for us to understand at first. We just don't speak the way they did in Elizabethan England. So what's the best way to approach

*Jeffery Wright as Mark Antony in Shakespeare's* Julius Caesar, *Delacorte Theater (2000)*

Shakespeare's plays? Steven Maler, artistic director of Commonwealth Shakespeare Company in Boston, Massachusetts, says that before you tackle the intricacies of the language, you need to understand what's actually going on and have a grasp of the settings and characters. One good way is to take a particular scene and improvise the action in your own words. Let's say you choose *Romeo and Juliet,* a perennial favorite.

How about a portion of act 1, scene 3, where Juliet's mother, Lady Capulet, informs her not-yet-fourteen-year-old daughter that Paris, a young

count whom Juliet has never laid eyes on, wants to marry her and she is to meet him that evening at a family party? She tells Juliet that women younger than she are already married with children, and that she herself was a mother at fourteen. Lady Capulet, referred to as "Wife" in the playscript, then describes at great length how incredibly attractive Paris is and, wasting no time, asks

*(continued on next page)*

*Patrick Stewart as Prospero in Shakespeare's* The Tempest, *Broadhurst Theater (1995)*

*(Time Out, continued)*

**Juliet if she is pleased by the idea of Paris's love. Poor Juliet, more than a bit overwhelmed, agrees to look at him to see if that will provoke affection but balks at anything more amorous. Also in this ensemble scene is Nurse, a lovable, opinionated, and impetuous woman who has cared for Juliet since her birth. She, too, is eager for Juliet to marry Paris, describing him as "a man of wax," Shakespearean lingo for handsome.**

Nurse: A man, young lady!
    Lady, such a man
As all the world—why, he's a
    man of wax.
Wife: Verona's summer hath
    not such a flower.
Nurse: Nay, he's a flower; in
    faith, a very flower.
Wife: What say you? Can you
    love the gentleman?
This night you shall behold
    him at our feast;
Read o'er the volume of young
    Paris' face
And find delight writ there
    with beauty's pen;
Examine every married
    lineament,
And see how one another
    lends content,

And what obscured in this fair
    volume lies
Find written in the margent
    *[corner]* of his eyes.
This precious book of love,
    this unbound lover,
To beautify him, only lacks a
    cover.
The fish lives in the sea, and
    'tis much pride
For fair without the fair within
    to hide.
That book in many's eyes doth
    share the glory,
That in gold clasps locks in the
    golden story;
So shall you share all that he
    doth possess,
By having him, making your-
    self no less.
Nurse: No less? Nay, bigger.
    Women grow by men.
Wife: Speak briefly, can you
    like of Paris' love?
Juliet: I'll look to like, if look-
    ing liking move:

But no more deep will I endart
    mine eye
Than your consent give
    strength to make it fly.

**Once you get the gist of the scene, read it through several more times to absorb its rhythms, then find a partner and improvise the exchange between Juliet and her mother in your own words. (Here's a chance to use your imagination big time.) Since you probably don't have a nurse in your life, make it a dialogue about something that relates to your own life. Take a look at the sample below for ideas as to how you might turn Shakespeare's words into a discussion that you might have with your own mother. Pay attention to what happens in the improv and try to find the connecting points between your scene and Shakespeare's.**

**Mother:** I got a call from Joe's mother today. They're planning a party for his bar mitzvah. He'd love you to come.

**Daughter:** Eeew. I hate Joe. He's dumb.

**Mother:** What do you mean, "dumb"? He's a nice boy.

**Daughter:** Um, no. He's a complete geek.

**Mother:** Come on. What's he ever done to you?

**Daughter:** All he does is sit by himself and study and read and stuff. He doesn't talk to me. I don't know why he wants me to go to his party.

**Mother:** Well, how about going just to be nice, since it is such a big day for him?

**Daughter:** But none of my friends are going.

**Mother:** Okay, but I know you don't want to hurt his feelings.

**Daughter:** Fine. I'll go. Whatever.

**How do the two overlap? You'll find the heartbeat and motivation of the scene through a process of discovery and investigation.**

**The following monologue (from act 2, scene 2) by a love-struck Romeo takes place in the Capulets' orchard. He is hiding from his friends, who want him to go home to bed, when he sees Juliet at a window in the balcony above.**

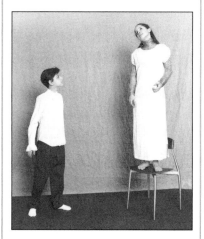

But, soft! what light through
   yonder window breaks?
It is the east, and Juliet is the
   sun.
Arise, fair sun, and kill the
   envious moon,
Who is already sick and pale
   with grief,
That thou her maid art far
   more fair than she:
Be not her maid, since she is
   envious;
Her vestal livery is but sick
   and green
And none but fools do wear it;
   cast it off.
It is my lady, O, it is my love!
O, that she knew she were!
She speaks yet she says
   nothing: what of that?
Her eye discourses; I will
   answer it.
I am too bold, 'tis not to me
   she speaks:
Two of the fairest stars in all
   the heaven,
Having some business, do
   entreat her eyes
To twinkle in their spheres till
   they return.
What if her eyes were there,
   they in her head?
The brightness of her cheek
   would shame those stars,
As daylight doth a lamp; her
   eyes in heaven
Would through the airy region
   stream so bright
That birds would sing and
   think it were not night.
See, how she leans her cheek
   upon her hand!
O, that I were a glove upon
   that hand,
That I might touch that cheek!

**These are the words of a young man falling in love. He is infatuated with Juliet, and declares that her beauty makes the moon envious and fills the stars with shame. Can you put Romeo's passionate words and feelings into your own?**

**It's helpful to know that the plays were written to be**

*(continued on next page)*

*(Time Out, continued)*

performed, not simply to be appreciated as literature. Though the language is beautiful to read, and packed with wonderful images, the play-script itself is a blueprint for the production. The more you read Shakespeare out loud and, best of all, see and hear it performed, the more you'll understand what he was all about. You'll find that there's an amazing structure to his verse, and when you start to probe and decode it, you'll form a deeper understanding and appreciation of Shakespeare's characters.

In addition to the tragic *Romeo and Juliet,* Steven Maler suggests a few comedies that might be especially appealing. *A Midsummer Night's Dream,* a wonderfully twisting and turning tale about young people rebelling against authority, takes place in an imaginary forest complete with fairies, transformations, and hilarious mix-ups (thanks mostly to the hopelessly confused Puck, the mischief-making clown of fairyland). *As You Like It* also has a forest, called the Forest of Arden. Though there are no magical creatures roaming around,

Arden brims with a collection of wonderfully comedic country folk. At its center is Rosalind, an intelligent and powerful female character often referred to as a female Hamlet. And it has the famous "All the world's a stage and all the men and women merely players" speech. *Twelfth Night,* which deals with issues of loneliness and separation from family, mistaken identities, and the triumph of true love, has two wonderful characters: the happy-go-lucky, happily corpulent Sir Toby Belch (!) and the bungling knight Sir Andrew Aguecheek.

*Orson Welles as the Moor with his Desdemona (Suzanne Cloutier) in* Othello *(1952)*

One of Shakespeare's strengths is the timelessness, and flexibility, of his plays. Many have been made into movies, which offer opportunities to see the plays in motion and provide a window into the almost infinite ways that his work can be interpreted. Some are historically accurate in terms of their settings and costumes. Others are reimagined for today's world, with the actors in modern-day clothing and environments.

When you compare a film to the play as Shakespeare wrote it, you'll discover that the directors chose to rearrange or leave out certain parts and expand upon others. Different film versions of the same play will have totally distinct looks and feelings. Here are some that you'll want to check out:

## Comedies

*As You Like It* (1936, directed by Paul Czinner, with Sir Laurence Olivier)

*A Midsummer Night's Dream* (1935, directed by Max Reinhardt; 1999, directed by Michael Hoffman, with Michelle Pfeiffer and Kevin Kline)

*Much Ado About Nothing* (1993, directed by Kenneth Branagh)

*Twelfth Night* (1996, directed by Trevor Nunn)

## Tragedies

*Hamlet* (1948, directed by Sir Laurence Olivier; 1969, directed by Tony Richardson; 2000, modern-day version directed by Michael Almereyda, with Ethan Hawke and Kyle MacLachlan)

*Romeo and Juliet* (1963, directed by George Cukor; 1968, directed by Franco Zeffirelli; 1996, modern-day version directed by Baz Lurmann, with Leonardo DiCaprio, Claire Danes, and John Leguizamo)

*Othello* (1952, directed by Orson Welles; 1965, directed by Stuart Burge; 1995, directed by Oliver Parker, with Laurence Fishburne)

## Histories

*Richard III* (1955, directed by Sir Laurence Olivier; 1995, directed by Richard Loncraine)

*Henry V* (1944, directed by Sir Laurence Olivier; 1989, directed by Kenneth Branagh)

And, of course, there's *Shakespeare in Love* (1998, directed by John Madden). It's not a dramatization of one of the Bard's plays, but a charming and imaginative look at his life, and the financial and artistic pressures on him to churn out his latest play, *Romeo and Ethel.* The rest, as they say, is history.

## The Globe Theatre

In Shakespeare's day everyone, except the very poor, went to the theater. It was the major source of entertainment: television, radio, movies, and video games were still several centuries away. Many plays were performed at London's Globe Theatre, a 3,000-seat theater whose open-air design left much of it vulnerable to the elements. In other words, if it rained you probably got wet.

The theater used flags of different colors to announce the type of play being performed: white meant a comedy; black, a tragedy; and red, a history. After being transported to the Globe by ferry across the Thames River, theatergoers dropped their admission into a box (the origin of the term "box office") and clambered to their seats. The cheapest seats (equivalent to a day's wages for a laborer) weren't seats at all, but an area at the front of the stage, known as "the yard," where the "groundlings" stood

*(continued on next page)*

and looked up at the stage. The wealthier patrons sat on benches, in one of three tiers that rose around the back. There was no scenery to speak of, and the actors entered and exited through an opening in a curtain that stretched across the middle of the stage. Since there was no lighting (the electric lightbulb wasn't invented until 1878), plays were performed at midday to take advantage of the sunlight.

Because the theater never got dark, people in the audience chatted with one another during the performances and interacted with the action onstage. Some Shakespeare scholars think— but no one knows for sure— that the audience responded to what they thought was a bad performance by pelting the actors with apples, hazelnuts, oranges, and gingerbread, the "popcorn" equivalents of the Elizabethan era. Professional male actors and boy apprentices, who portrayed female roles until their voices changed, played all the parts. Women were not allowed onstage.

Shakespeare was one of several playwrights whose works were performed at the Globe, and it was during a 1613 production of his *King Henry VIII* that a spark from a cannon announcing the king's entrance set the timber-frame structure on fire, quickly burning it to the ground. After a hasty reconstruction in 1614, the Globe continued operations until 1642, when theater-shunning Puritans shut it down, along with every other theater in town. Shortly afterward, it was demolished to make way for housing. In 1997, on roughly the same site as the original theater, the New Globe was inaugurated with an all-male performance of *King Henry V,* a historical play Shakespeare wrote in 1599, the year the Old Globe Theatre first opened.

*An artist's rendering of the Globe Theater, drawn in the late 1700s*

# chapter eight

# Backstage Pass

*Stage Managers • Set Designs • Props • Lighting • Stage Lingo •*
*Kinds of Theaters • Dolby Sound • Special Effects •*
*Costuming • Makeup • Masks*

The unique and magical way that a production looks and sounds is the result of close collaborations between the director and the set, lighting, sound, costume, and makeup designers. They create the world in which the characters live. All of this creativity needs to be organized, a job that falls to the stage manager, who makes sure that everything happens according to plan and on cue with maximum efficiency and minimum fuss. Since this role is so pivotal, let's start there.

# Stage Manager

Do you love to make lists? Are you a fanatic about where you stash your stuff? Can you talk on the phone, eat a snack, listen to music, and do your homework all at the same time, without missing a beat? Are you the calm one when everyone around you is freaking out? Are you a natural problem solver? If you answer yes to at least two of these questions, you just might be cut out to be a stage manager, the person whose job it is to manage the stage and everything and everyone that goes on and off it.

Think of an old-fashioned wagon wheel. You are like the hub, processing information that comes in on the wheel's spokes, then sending it out again. The information has to do with organizing the actors, the director, the tech crew, and the designers—so everyone has time to do the work he or she needs to do and in a sequence that makes sense. An actor cannot rehearse a scene that takes place on stairs unless the stairs, or something representing the stairs, are in place. The lighting designer cannot cue the lights until the lights are hung. The sound person cannot check sound levels if the carpenters are making a racket installing a set. The janitor cannot turn on the house lights in the middle of a dress rehearsal to clean the seats. And since there is never enough time for each person to do what has to be done without anyone else around to get in the way, you have to figure out which things can happen at the same time.

So how is it done? Do you grab a bullhorn and shout out directions? Not exactly.

**1.** You start by creating a production schedule before the rehearsals actually begin; then you negotiate with all concerned and try to make accommodations or adjustments where possible.

**2.** Once rehearsals begin, you coordinate and monitor the **load-in** and set up, keeping track of everything and everyone.

**3.** You also keep the book for the director: what the actors are doing, including all the blocking notes. You might be doing this in a studio or onstage, depending on where rehearsals are held.

**4.** By the time production week rolls around (just before opening night), you're in the theater full-time. And it's a scheduling nightmare. Everyone wants as much time as possible, and these times almost always conflict. Here's where your superior powers of organization and diplomacy really get a workout.

**5.** Now, finally, it's opening night and the show is turned over to you. You are in charge.

**6.** You call all the cues: when the curtain opens, when the lights come up, when the sound cues happen.

**7.** And you make sure the actors are onstage at the right time. In addition to all of this, a big part of your job is being able to anticipate and deal with problems as they occur. This doesn't mean you have to be a mind reader, though a bit of ESP wouldn't hurt.

What can go wrong? Well, just about everything, from a tape recorder not working to a power failure (oops, all the lights went out!) to a curtain getting stuck halfway up (it happens!) to an actor paralyzed by stage fright in the wings. You have to find a way out of these sticky situations as quickly and gracefully as possible. Let's say the curtain is stuck halfway open and the actors are onstage. You might fade the stage lights out, get the actors offstage, then bring the house

**load-in:** the process of bringing the sets, props, scenery, and costumes into the theater

lights up to half and announce to the audience that you're fixing the problem and to please be patient. Then you go to work to see if the curtain can actually be fixed. If the curtain can't be opened (remember, your audience is waiting, not all that patiently), you might take a couple of ropes and pull it up on either side, creating what's known as a "swag effect." And instead of having the curtain open and close to signify beginnings and endings, you might have the lights go up and down. Once that's done (whew!), you need to find a logical point where the play can start again. Now, about those poor actors. . . .

How do you keep from panicking? Experience, patience, and a great sense of humor. Ha, ha! In theater, emotions are heightened, and people are tense, excited, and temperamental. **You need to be a sea of calm in the storm.** If you get excited, this raises the confusion. Your job is to pull the level of tension down so people can do what they need to do.

• You have to put yourself in a state of awareness, keep yourself open. If you become too rigid about certain ways of doing things, something will trip up your system.

• You have to be flexible and able to adjust minute by minute. It helps if you have done other jobs backstage.

• A working knowledge of technical work is essential.

• A bit of acting experience is always an advantage. If you have performed, you understand stage fright. To a certain extent it's easier to be a dictator, but you cannot force a good performance. You can't say to an actor, "You *will* act well now!" What you can do is set up conditions so it can be done.

• As stage manager, you are a mechanic, general, counselor, and, let's not forget, saint, all rolled into one.

# Make a Scene

## Rig a Curtain

You're putting on a show at home and want to have a proper stage curtain. No problem. You need just a few things:

• A doorway from which to hang your curtain, and through which you will enter and exit. (Be sure there's room for audience seating on one side, since your stage will need to be in front of one side of the curtain.)

• Two old bedsheets or lightweight blankets.

• A broom or mop handle. (You may need to cut one or tape two together to get the right length.)

• Two big mug hooks that can handle the weight of the rod *AND* your curtain.

• A stepladder or very sturdy chair.

• Six to eight clip-on curtain rings—the kind that grip the fabric.

After getting the parental okay to proceed:

1. Attach the mug hooks to the top two corners of the doorway opening that faces the audience.

2. Rest the curtain rod across the hooks.

3. Slip the curtain rings over the handle and place it on the hooks.

4. Hang the sheets or blankets from the curtain rings; use three or four for each one.

Voilà! You're in business. If you wish to create a dramatic swag effect, you can tie back the curtains on each side with colorful ribbons or rope. And if the sheets or blankets are truly old (that is, not to be used on beds ever again!), you might decorate them with fabric paints or glitter.

## I Need a Ming Vase, Pronto!

The set designer's responsibilities include choosing and often designing props—all of the "stuff" that makes a stage or film environment feel authentic. Props, short for properties, include large items like sofas, tables, and pianos, and smaller objects like telephones, paintings, and coffee cups. They are often divided into categories according to their size. A hand property, for example, includes anything that

is carried or handled by the actors: books, pencils, hairbrushes, etc.

Larger theatrical productions often have a prop master, the person who takes care of tracking down or supervising the construction of the props. Furniture may need to be built or reupholstered. Sometimes prop elements are created out of papier-mâché, a lightweight pulpy material made from paper, water, and wheat paste that can be molded into elaborate shapes. Often a designer or prop master will pay a visit to the local prop house, a business totally devoted to renting props. They tend to be in larger cities, and are packed with all sorts of odd and wonderful things. Anyone need a vintage jukebox?

# What Does It Mean to Call a Show?

During rehearsal and setting up, the director and the lighting and sound designers make cues. As stage manager, you need to know where and when each cue happens and who needs to execute it. When does that piece of scenery roll away? How about that prop, where does it go? Doesn't this actor belong onstage now? Does the curtain close at this point? You need to mark every cue so when it's time to call the show, you are prepared. You'll keep track of time with your trusty stopwatch.

When you call a show, you not only need to tell each person when to do his or her thing, you first need to warn everyone so they're prepared. You start calling the show before the performance actually begins. There's the "half-hour" call, which lets the cast and crew know that the show is set to begin in thirty minutes. The actors should be in the final stages of getting dressed, made up, and warmed up. The crew should be confirming that the props, set pieces, and equipment are in place. At this point the audience begins to stream in and get seated. This is usually followed by "fifteen minutes," "five minutes," and "places," which literally means "Get in place. It's show time!"

Warnings happen throughout the show, for every single cue. The sound person needs to keep a finger on his or her tape machine. The curtain person needs to be next to the rope, ready to pull. The props have to be put in place so they can be carried onstage. You will give a warning, in a logical order, to whoever is involved. Then, when the action is ready to happen, you have to remember to cue each person to go, at the right moment. Curtain, go. Light cue one, go. Sound, go. Some people might be cued from a command you speak into your headset. Or a "Go" hissed at them in the wings. Others, if a verbal cue isn't possible, watch for a gesture, like pointing, or cue lights: a little blue or red light may be used to cue an actor on the other side of the stage, for example. When it comes on, it's time to get ready. When it goes off, it's time to go. As shows become more complicated, four to five things might have to happen at the same time. No problem! You are calm and organized.

# Set Design

Take a look around your bedroom. There's a bed, maybe a shelf filled with books, and a desk and a chair. You might have a huge pile of dirty laundry creating a roadblock in the middle of the

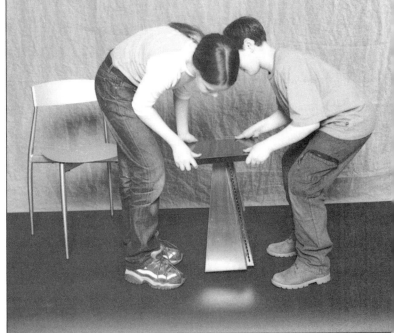

floor. If there's a window, it may have a shade or a curtain. Open it and you can see your backyard or perhaps a city street. Now imagine your bedroom, mess and all, transferred onto a stage.

If you were a **set** designer, you would make a habit of transforming real as well as fantastic settings into theater. You would scrutinize the script to learn as much as possible about the characters and how they live. Where and when does the play take place? If it's set in a home, are the owners wealthy

**set:** an environment created onstage that establishes the atmosphere, era, and location of the play

or poor? What style of furniture do the inhabitants have? What do the walls of their living room look like? Are they covered with ornate wallpaper and old photographs, or are they white and empty? Is there a tea set or a pile of books on the coffee table? Is there a coffee table?

Whatever you choose to put on the stage has to be there for a reason. Unless there is a conscious effort on the part of the director to reimagine the play in another time or place, the set and all of the props, no matter how small, should reflect the intentions of the script. If it's set in the Victorian

*A ground plan by scenic designer Venustiano Borromeo for* The Merchant of Venice

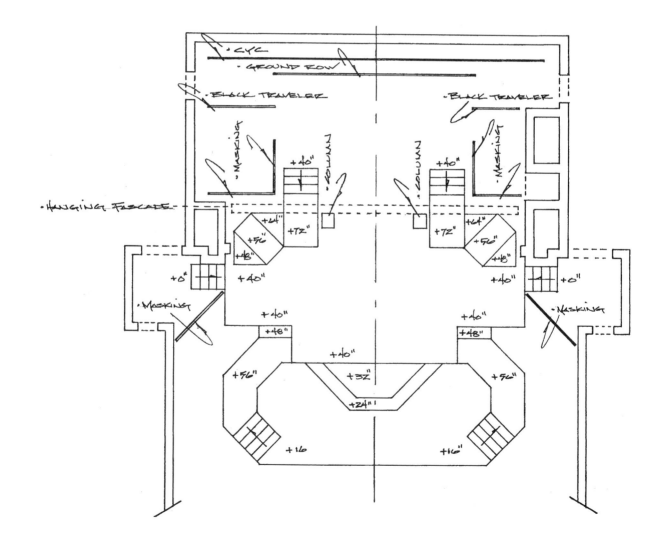

*A scene design for* The Merchant of Venice, *first as a drawing (top), then as a realized set in the theater*

era, the furniture, rugs, and decorations should suggest 1870s England, not 1960s America.

After discussing the overall design concept with the director, the set designer makes some sketches of the scenery and props and may also find photographs that evoke an emotional response. He or she meets with the director again and makes adjustments. The designer then creates blueprints—similar to the drawings an architect makes—and a model of each set that can be interpreted by the scene shop. (Take a look at a dollhouse to get a rough idea of what a scale model looks like.) The models are made of balsa wood, mat board, or Fome-Cor, and designed to scale. You know how many maps use one inch to equal one mile? A set designer's blueprints might use $1/2$ inch to equal one foot in real life.

The designer considers not only what the set looks like but also how it functions on the stage with the actors moving through it. If you were designing Shakespeare's *A Midsummer Night's Dream*, for example, you would probably think twice before filling the stage with lots of little twiggy trees that would certainly snag the fairies' gauzy, flowing gowns.

The set designer's job often starts before rehearsals. It would be hard for a director to block a show if he or she didn't know where the doors or stairs were going to be. If the set isn't completed before rehearsals begin, the set elements will be marked on the stage from the "ground plan" (a bird's-eye-view drawing of the stage) and the "section," a drawing that shows how tall things are and where they are in relation to one another and to the theater itself.

*A set by Venustiano Borromeo for* Fifth of July, *as imagined in a drawing (left), then brought to life in the theater (right)*

*Set and costume designs by Venustiano Borromeo for* The Mikado

To get an idea of what this means, imagine taking hold of the world's biggest chain saw and cutting your kitchen in half from top to bottom. For example, the slice might show how much space there is between the top of the refrigerator and the ceiling. This information is useful when deciding where to hang lights and place scenery.

These drawings are also used to indicate **sight lines,** the angles at which people sitting in the audience see the stage (see page 156). The idea is to make a complete environment, a world that the audience thinks goes on forever.

The set designer's work doesn't stop at the drawing board.

He or she is always around during load-in, when the set is brought onto the stage, to make sure everything is okay. If it doesn't fit, the designer wants to be there to be sure that some important element isn't chopped off. **Depending on the size and budget of a production, the set designer sometimes actually builds the set.** During tech rehearsals the set designer is in charge of how the scenery should move. Often scene changes happen in front of the audience, making the scenery as much a part of the show as the performers are.

Unlike the color wheel you studied in school, the light color wheel's primary colors are not red, yellow, and blue. They're red, yellow, and green. Wait just a minute, you say, green is a secondary color, a combination of blue and yellow! This is true when you're working with pigment colors (used in materials like crayons, pencils, paints, and markers). Light behaves very differently. If you mix all of the pigment colors together, you get black, or something close to it. Mix the primary light colors together and you get (surprise!) white light. Yes, you do.

But there's more. Not all white light is the same. It can be warm or cool. Old-fashioned incandescent light gives off a warm yellowish glow that gets yellower as it is dimmed down. The halogen bulb in a desk lamp radiates a harsh cool blue light. Fluorescent lights make your eyes tired because they don't have all the colors.

**dimmer board:** a machine that controls the light cues

**gels:** small sheets of colored plastic that are slipped in front of a bulb to give the beam color and texture

# Lighting Design

Let there be light! When used skillfully onstage, light can turn night to day, create a mood through color, angle, texture, and intensity, and even shape the space an actor occupies.

Stage light is very different from light in the real world. In the real world, if it's a sunny day, light seems to be everywhere: in the treetops, on the lawn, buildings, and sidewalks. Turn on the lights in your house and the whole place gets bright. This is known as **general illumination.** In the theater, light is supercontrolled so that it hits a certain person or thing but doesn't touch something else. Even shadows, the natural partners of light, can be made to disappear. This is known as **selective visibility:** choosing what is or isn't seen. The effects can be realistic or totally fantastic. Try this for a quick demo: grab a flashlight, turn out all the lights, and stand in front of a mirror. Now, holding the flashlight directly under your chin, shine the beam up toward your face. Spooky! All those shadows make you look positively ghoulish.

Some theaters are outfitted with a vast array of sophisticated lights and a gigantic computerized **dimmer board.** Others manage with a handful of basic lights and **gels.** If you're really clever, you can create dazzling results with just a few carefully directed beams. It all starts with a **light plot.**

There are four major elements in lighting:

**1. Intensity:** This is the strength of the light in proportion to what's around it. If you take a flashlight outside on a sunny day and turn it on, you can barely see the beam. But take that same flashlight into a pitch black room and turn it on, and the beam will be blindingly bright.

**2. Movement:** This means a few things: the process of light getting brighter or darker (called *dimming up* or *dimming down*), the motion of a *follow spot* (a strong beam of light that literally follows a performer around the stage), and the *pacing* of the light cues (how frequently the lights go on and off). Too many light changes can become monotonous and irritating, and too few can be disorienting. The light should serve the play, not be the focus of it.

**3. Distribution:** This is the angle and shape of the light beams. You know how an upward beam from your flashlight casts weird shadows on your face. Shine a light directly down from the top of your head, and you get another set of equally creepy shadows. Shine it from the side, and one half of your face is lit while the other half disappears in shadow. (**Sidelighting** is often used to light dancers because it models, or shapes, the body.)

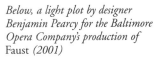

**light plot:** a drawing that looks a lot like an architect's blueprint, but instead of indicating where a door or window might go, it shows where in a particular theater each light should be hung

*Below, a light plot by designer Benjamin Pearcy for the Baltimore Opera Company's production of* Faust *(2001)*

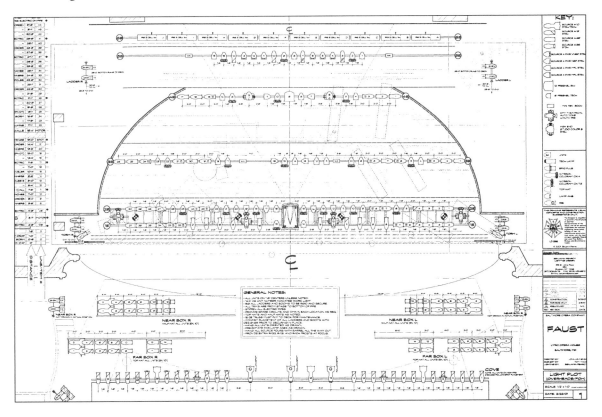

Play with different angles and you'll begin to get an idea of how a slight shift can drastically change how you look. Designers usually use a combination of angles and beams.

**4. Color:** This is tricky. It doesn't mean the same thing to everyone. Green might mean envy, peace and calm, or money. How is that green going to be used and what is it going to hit? The costumes, the set, the floor, someone's skin? Certain shades of green on white people make them look sick. Yet that same shade gives black skin a lovely glow. You've probably noticed that if you stare at one color too long, it starts to lose impact; your eyes grow tired. So, for example, if you want the backdrop on your stage to be really blue, you need to add a splotch of red for contrast, to keep the blue alive. Different effects are achieved depending on your light source, whether or not you use gels, and the color of the surface that you are lighting.

There are three basic types of theatrical lights:

**1. Leko:** a strong, sharp-edged beam that passes through a curved mirror.

*Below are examples of uplighting and sidelighting.*

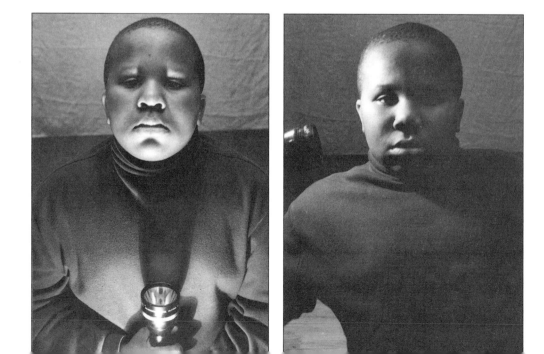

**2. Fresnel:** based on a lens developed by a Frenchman (Augustin-Jean Fresnel) for lighthouses. It is a spotlight, hot (which means bright) in the middle but with a soft edge.

**3. Cyclorama:** a floodlight, used for a wash of light over a huge defined area. It doesn't have a lens, just a curved mirror that aims the light onto a specific surface.

Special equipment like **barn doors** (not real doors, but a contraption that attaches to the light and swings open and shut), **shutters** (a tiny version of what's on a window), **extended snouts** (think long hollow nose), and **tape** can also be used to control the width and shape of the beam.

# Sound Design

Sound check! Testing, testing. One, two, three, testing. A sound operator is constantly testing, adjusting, and testing again. This very patient person may, depending on the size of a production, also be the sound designer, who is responsible for devising and recording sound effects and providing any amplification that may be required.

After reading the script several times and consulting with the director, the sound designer creates a **sound plot.** This is an intricate chart that notes where in the script sound cues occur and what they are. Often sounds are recorded, then played back through the theater's sound system. And sometimes they are "performed" live. Since live and recorded sounds have very distinct qualities, it's tricky to mix the two. Our ears can tell the difference. See for yourself. Record the sound of water running in your shower and play it back. How does it sound? Now turn on the shower and listen to the gushing "live." How do the two versions compare?

The sound designer deals with much more than special effects. Sometimes actors wear tiny mikes (shorthand for microphones) in their hair or tucked into their costumes. These are called "beltpacks." A thin cable runs down the back of the actor's neck, through his or her clothing, into a small battery pack worn at the waist. **An actor gets wired while dressing.** After he or she is in costume, guess what happens? You got it. Another test! Beltpack batteries, along with any others that might be in handheld mikes or part of the ClearCom system, must be changed and tested before every single performance. "ClearCom system" refers to the headsets that have mikes that swing in front of the mouth. The stage manager wears one and so does everyone he or she needs to communicate with during the show.

*At right, an audio console speaker plot by Michael Creason and Mark Bennett for* Dogeaters, *by Jessica Hagedorn, at the Joseph Papp Public Theater, New York Shakespeare Festival (2001)*

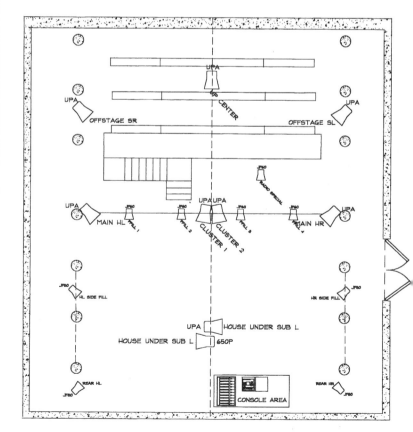

| 104 | Preshow Radio | 1 | |
| 104.1 | Preshow Fade up | | |
| 106 | Opening Tuning | 1 | |
| 115 | Short Tuning/ Long Tuning Bed | 1 | |
| 201 | Short Tuning 2 | 1 | |
| 206 | Short Tuning 3 | 1 | |
| 210 | Short Tuning 4 | 1 | |
| 215 | Short Tuning 5 | 1 | |
| 301 | Short Tuning 6 | 1 | |
| 303 | Short Tuning 7 | 1 | |
| 306 | Multi Guns/Variety Music 1 | 1 | |
| 306.6 | Variety Intro FADE | 2 | |
| 315 | Timp Roll/ Variety OUT | 2 | |
| 401 | The Survivor Music/Shower USL | 2 | |
| 406 | Rivet Stroke/Music OUT | 3 | |
| 410 | The Beauty Queen "aaah" | 3 | |
| 415 | The Penitent | 3 | |
| 501 | The Exile | 3 | |
| 506 | Gunshots | 3 | |
| 510 | Torrid Zone | 3 | |
| 512 | Torrid Zone OUT | 3 | |
| 516 | Mallat Mic ON | 4 | |
| 601 | Mallat Reverie | 5 | |
| 602 | Mallat OUT | | |

*Left, a* Dogeaters *sound plot packed with cues*

Sometimes mikes are not battery operated but connected to a "hard" wire. These are obviously less desirable than a wireless system when there are great distances between the mike and the outlet or when a performer has to move around a lot. **Think about the tangles a twirling actor could get into!** But there are drawbacks to wireless mikes, too. It's not uncommon for them to go dead in the middle of a scene. Sweat is a major culprit. All that moisture tends to short-circuit the unit. If this happens, the actor must soldier on bravely (and loudly) until he or she can exit and the unit can be switched. Putting the beltpack in a plastic bag can often prevent this problem.

What sounds good in rehearsal won't necessarily sound good at all during performance, not because the performers are speaking too loudly or softly but because the number of people sitting in the audience in their heavy winter coats has drastically affected the sound levels. You know how a recording studio has padded walls to absorb the sound? Bodies and clothing act as absorbent padding. If the theater is packed with people (always a happy event), the sound will be more muffled than during rehearsals, when no one but the director and a few others were sitting in the house.

Another reason for adjustments might be if performers are dancing and breathing heavily. A sound operator will want to take the distracting sound of an actor's panting out of the mix by lowering the volume on her mike until she catches her breath.

# Backstage Lingo

As you're discovering, the stage has its own set of rules and the lingo to go with them. It also has wonderful words to describe the various objects that float above and surround it. Not every stage has the same stuff, of course. How it's outfitted depends on its shape, size, and the sorts of productions that it serves. Impress your fellow thespians with this starter list of backstage technospeak.

**Batten.** Some stage lights and the curtain are hung from a batten, which is a metal pipe that hangs from the top of the fly space. Sometimes the batten is suspended from "lift lines," cables or ropes that can be raised or lowered.

**Beamport.** This is an opening in the ceiling above the audience where additional stage lights can be hung.

# Stages Come in Many Sizes and Shapes

In addition to proscenium stages, there are several other types that offer directors, performers, designers, and audiences distinctly different theatrical challenges and experiences. Below are a few of the most common.

*Theater-in-the-round.* Also known as an arena, a theater-in-the-round is a stage surrounded by the audience on all sides. This requires that the action be directed all around. These stages usually have very simple sets, which make sense (and don't block views) no matter where someone is seated. A theater-in-the-round doesn't use upstage, downstage, etc., but instead describes its directions in reference to the aisles as if they're on a giant clock face. Twelve o'clock is usually the aisle closest to the location of the technical equipment controls. The aisle opposite would then be 6 o'clock and the two on either side (halfway between 12 and 6) 3 o'clock and 9 o'clock. See the photo on the next page to get an idea.

*Thrust stage.* In a thrust theater, the audience sits on three sides. The stage action extends beyond the fourth wall of the proscenium, onto the "apron" of the stage, the part in front of the curtain line that "thrusts" into the audience. As with a theater-in-the-round, the thrust stage requires sets that work from more than one direction.

*Black box.* This is a modern, flexible theater that can be converted into several types of stages, including arena, thrust, and proscenium. Sometimes the audience is seated on two sides and the action happens in the middle. The space itself is often painted black to mask any distracting features of the room. The lighting and sets are basic, and performances tend to be informal and often experimental, with the exciting feeling of a workshop. The audience feels as if it is part of something fresh and on the "cutting edge."

*All the world's a stage.* Sometimes performances are presented in the great outdoors. The stage might be a platform or tent plopped down in the middle of a field, or it might be a huge green lawn, a parking lot, or even a city street. These performances tend to be more informal and experimental, and often break down the traditional barrier between the audience and the performers. (See Avant-garde Theater: What Is It?, page 96.)

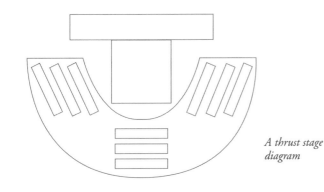

*A thrust stage diagram*

*Above, from top to bottom: a black box stage, an outdoor performance, and theater-in-the-round (see page 155)*

**Drops.** Often elaborately painted cloths that set a scene or establish a mood and are hung from the fly space. A single production may have just one drop or dozens.

**Fly space.** High up above the proscenium is the fly space, a space where lighting equipment, scenery, backcloths, and drops can be "flown"—hidden from view or stored until needed.

**Gridiron.** An iron grid from which scenery and lights are hung. It is like a giant open floor high above the stage.

**Pit.** Most proscenium-type stages have a pit, a space between the stage and the first row of the audience's seating where musicians sit and play. In some theaters the pit is actually an elevator floor that can be raised up to the level of the stage to create a "thrust": a portion of the stage, also called an "apron," that "thrusts" into the audience. (See Thrust stage, page 155.)

**Rigging.** The act of rigging is the complex process of hanging scenery and lights; the term also refers to the ropes and the gridiron that they are hung from. Rigging of the rigging (!) happens, ideally, before the technical rehearsals.

**Sight lines.** Designers and directors pay close attention to sight lines because they refer to what the audience can or cannot see from various seats in the house. They need to be sure that no one sitting far left, for example, will accidentally catch a glimpse of a stagehand drinking coffee in the wings off stage left, or miss a crucial bit of action or a piece of scenery that is beyond view. Horizontal sight lines correspond to the seats farthest to the right and to the left. Vertical sight lines correspond to the seats that are in the front row of the audience and the last row of the balcony or, if there isn't a balcony, the very last row of the orchestra (the "ground floor" of the house). Rule of thumb for actors: if you can see them, they can see you.

**Teasers and tormentors.** Sound like the words you use to describe your brother or sister? Actually, teasers and tormentors have nothing to do with sibling torture. They are nifty adjustable frames that can change the size of a proscenium opening. A teaser runs along the top and can be lowered to reduce the proscenium's height. Tormentors run vertically along the right and left sides and can reduce the width of the opening. They are also used to mask backstage equipment or activity that might otherwise be seen from "the house" (audience).

**Wings.** These are the areas offstage right and left where actors make entrances and exits and from where scenery and props can be moved on- and offstage. Some theaters have wings with ample room for several people and props (depending on how large they are), while others are barely big enough to accommodate a single actor.

# Bells and Whistles

Onstage you see a woman reading in her living room. She's sitting on a sofa. A couple of armchairs, a lamp, and a coffee table piled with books and magazines complete the decor. Nothing seems out of the ordinary. Until you hear a door suddenly slam shut. Somewhere, glass shatters, followed by a gunshot and hurried footsteps crunching along a path. What's happening here? What crime? It's all in your mind. In your ears, actually. The slamming door came from a wooden box with a hinged top and an assortment of racket-making latches, chains, and bolts. A window didn't break. That was a pane of glass being (carefully) smashed inside a

*A Foley artist simulates the sound of a person walking outdoors (above) and a crackling fire (below).*

padded crate. Those mysterious footsteps were produced by someone walking quickly across a tray filled with gravel. And there was no gun, smoking or otherwise. That loud *POP!* came from a stagehand bending, then abruptly releasing a plank of wood. Don't try this one at home. These noises are known in the theater as *sound effects* or SFX, and their impact depends on a delicate balance of imagination and skill. The people who create sound effects for film are known as Foley artists.

Surprising effects as well as familiar background sounds—the rumbling of traffic, for example—can also be generated by special equipment designed to duplicate, amplify, or invent sound, like tape recorders (reel-to-reel tapes provide the truest sound), loudspeakers, microphones, and of course synthesizers. Whether assembled from stuff around the house (swirl a cupful of dried beans around a kitchen sieve and you have the sound of rain) or manufactured by a sophisticated machine, the goal is the same: to use sound, a most vital theatrical element, that's heard but never seen, to help create a mood and a sense of place and drama.

Here are some more "fool the ear" sounds:

**Boiling water:** stick a straw into a glass of water and slowly blow bubbles

**Fire:** crunch and twist a piece of cellophane

**Squeaky car breaks:** turn a drinking glass upside down and slide it along a pane of glass

**Ripping:** pull apart two strips of Velcro

**Horse's hooves:** turn a couple of empty yogurt or margarine containers (throw away the lids) upside down and clip-clop them against a table top or gravel-filled tray

# Costume Design

They say that clothes make the man or woman. They certainly help make the character. Whether a play calls for worn-out jeans, a T-shirt, and a pair of beat-up tennis shoes or an ornate ball gown and headdress, a costume designer works along with the director and the set and lighting designers to place an actor in the proper dramatic context.

*Costume designs by Venustiano Borromeo for the New York Lyric Opera's production of* Abigail Adams

*Costumes and sets were elaborate in this production of* Hello, Dolly! *designed by Venustiano Borromeo.*

**A costume communicates vital information** about a character, including age, occupation, social status—even a state of mind. Look around at how people dress the next time you're out and about. What can you learn about people from their choices of clothing? What do their choices tell you about how they feel about themselves?

In addition to creating a strong identity for each character, costumes are a vital ingredient in the total visual stage

picture. They coordinate with the set and lighting design to establish a mood as well as a clear sense of time and place. You keep reading those two words, *time* and *place*. This is because, in addition to a playwright's use of language, the ways that designers interpret the way characters and their environments look and sometimes sound clue us in to *when* and *where* what we are seeing onstage is supposed to be happening.

★ **David** *Costumes make the show come alive and help you get into character. I don't really care about makeup.*

★ **Sophie** *Your costume can reveal information about your character to the audience that might not be in the script.*

Once the setting and time are established, the costume designer gets to work. This means researching books, magazines, photographs, and often paintings for ideas and historical guidance. How did people dress and what was going on during the period described in the play? Even if the costumes are based on an imaginary time and place, the designer may still look to these sources for inspiration.

A chart is useful to plot each character's movement through the play. What sort of clothing and accessories does each actor require? Who needs a coat, hat, boots, or maybe a parasol? How many times does each actor have to change costumes? And how much time does he or she have? If a change has to happen in a split second, a costume with dozens of buttons or laces will be a problem. When speed is of the essence, use snaps or Velcro! When this much has been mapped out, it's time to make sketches. Some designers make paintings, rich in color. Some make ink or pencil drawings. And others make collages layered with fabric samples and detailed instructions. It doesn't really matter what style of sketch the designer uses, as long as the costumes can be understood by the director and other designers and, of course, by the people who have to make them. In many productions, the designer of the costumes and the person who makes them are one and the same.

Before actually getting down to creating the patterns, cutting, and sewing, the costume designer will show the lighting designer the fabrics to be sure they work under the lights.

**Not all costumes are made from scratch.** In fact, in most productions the budget limitations demand that the

## EDITH HEAD

The great costume designer Edith Head (1899–1981) solved the "What do I wear?" question for more than one thousand movies. She once said, "What a costume designer does is a cross between magic and camouflage. We create the illusion of changing the actors into what they are not." Edith Head worked her magic on all kinds of costumes, from ultraglamorous gowns and tuxedos to dusty, beaten-up cowboy duds.

*Audrey Hepburn as the chic Holly Golightly in* Breakfast at Tiffany's *(1961)*

Here is a very short list of films that Edith Head outfitted during her long career:

*The Heiress* (1949)
*The Greatest Show on Earth* (1952)
*Houdini* (1953)
*Sabrina* (1954)
*Breakfast at Tiffany's* (1961)
*The Disorderly Orderly* (1964)
*Butch Cassidy and the Sundance Kid* (1969)
*The Sting* (1973)
*The Great Waldo Pepper* (1975)

designer be a bit of a scavenger. This can be lots of fun. Thrift shops, department stores, and the designer's and actors' own closets can be great sources for costumes. There is still plenty of room for creativity. A T-shirt can be spruced up with glitter. An old quilt can be cut up and resewn into a glamorous shawl or skirt. A frumpy pair of boots can be dyed or updated with a layer of fringe.

Costumes have to be fitted on the actors. This sounds simple, but given all of the technical demands of putting a show together, combined with the hectic pace of rehearsals, it's never easy. If you can manage to squeeze in a couple of fittings for every costume, you're doing well. These will give you a chance to make any necessary adjustments and soothe fragile actor egos (This makes me look fat! I can't breathe/walk in this!) in plenty of time for the dress rehearsal, when everything should be finished—or almost.

So, how do they look? Are the actors comfortable? Or as comfortable as anyone can be while wearing a mask and a heavy fur cape? How do the costumes work with the lights and the set? You will make only the necessary changes at this point. But even the few things you need to fix will take time, meaning you'll be cutting, basting, and fastening up to, and likely beyond, the opening curtain. But the costumes will be gorgeous!

# Hair and Makeup

A costume isn't complete without equal attention paid to hair and makeup. One role may require nothing more than a neatly combed "do" and a touch of foundation. Another may demand a wig, a prosthetic (fake) nose, and a gruesome scar. If your production is fortunate enough to have a makeup artist (many do not), this person will read the script, make notes about every character, and consult with the director and the rest of the show's designers to determine what sort of hair and makeup are required. Sometimes the designer will even apply the performers' "faces," though it's more likely, unless the makeup is supercomplicated, that the designer will show the actors what to do with the expectation that they'll watch and listen carefully and be able to do it on their own.

If you have ever worn a wig, you know how much fun it can be to try on a new look without having to dye your hair, get it cut, or wait for your locks to grow down to the middle of your back. Wigs, hairpieces, baldcaps, and fake beards and mustaches are a big part of creating a costume and character. If you wear a wig, it needs to fit comfortably so you are not distracted by its presence while per-forming: "Is that a squirrel sitting

**spirit gum:** a special glue made from alcohol, plant resin, and castor oil

⭐ **Sophie** *Practice putting on your makeup at home so you're comfortable using it.*

on my head?" The same goes for a mustache or beard: "There's a caterpillar slithering across my lips!"

The "hair" that these pieces are made of is actually a synthetic called "crepe" that is pretty easy to trim and shape. Facial hairpieces (beards, mustaches, eyebrows) are adhered to the skin with **spirit gum.** Most people can use it without a problem. But if your skin starts to itch or burn, remove it promptly (with spirit gum remover).

**Stage makeup can enhance your features** so the people sitting way back in Row Z get the full whammy of your natural good looks. It can also transform you from a fourteen-year-old boy into a ninety-five-year-old woman. Truly! And it can turn you from a normal-looking human kid into a bizarre-looking creature from a distant planet. No matter what you want stage makeup to do, if you want it to be effective, you need to study the geography of your face. "I already know what I look like," you say. Ha! You *think* you know your face well.

Yes, you stare at it in the mirror when you brush your teeth, and probably sneak a peek or two a few more times during the day. But do you know if it is heart-shaped, round, oval, or squarish? What about your lips? Are they thick, thin, or in-between? How about your eyebrows: bushy or pencil thin? Does your chin recede slightly, or maybe jut out a tad? Do you have a broad or narrow forehead? The more you understand all of the planes, nooks, and crannies that define your face, the more effectively you will be able to apply your makeup, no matter what sort of role you are playing. Makeup can help reveal aspects of your character, including age and state of physical and emotional health. Rosy cheeks and lips imply youth and physical

**Joey** In Beauty and the Beast, *the Beast has a glued-on nose and all this makeup. One night he was really sweating a lot and the nose slipped down slowly until it fell off his chin and onto the stage. He just bent down and picked it up and put it back on. I don't think the audience noticed, but I did.*

*Makeup and costume can achieve a number of different effects, from natural enhancements to complete makeovers.*

well-being, while runny mascara or smeared lipstick can send a message of distress.

There are basically four categories of stage makeup, and each requires a different approach:

**1. Straight** makeup aims to create a natural look onstage. But in a large theater, where the stage is relatively far away from the audience and the lights are extremely bright, if you wear no makeup at all your face will appear washed out. So to achieve the natural look, you need to enhance your features so they can be "read" from the back of the house. If the performance is in a small theater where the audience sits very close to the stage, actors going for a natural look may opt to wear virtually no makeup.

**2. Character** makeup exaggerates and dramatizes the features. You may be playing a character who is bald, sports a long gray beard, and is extremely old. Each of these features requires a skilled hand with the makeup kit.

**3. Stylized** makeup often projects a recognizable image of a particular character, like a witch (scraggly hair stuffed under a pointed black hat, a long, wart-speckled nose) or a clown (white face, red nose, painted-on grin, goofy hat). It also can be used in productions where the actors' faces are part of an overall design. In these cases, the designer will determine each performer's makeup.

**4. Fantastic** or **FX** (special effects) makeup—think *Star Trek, Star Wars,* and *X-Men*—aims to transform the actor into something else entirely. It is almost always designed and overseen by a makeup artist, and often includes

*Makeup works magic on Jim Carrey and costars in* Dr. Suess' How the Grinch Stole Christmas *(2000).*

all sorts of strange elements that have absolutely nothing to do with the structure of your own face or body. For the actor, the experience is more like wearing a mask or armor than makeup.

It's fun to experiment with makeup. If you can work in a bathroom with lights all around the mirror, that's ideal, because this mimics the kind of light that is on your face onstage. If you don't have that kind of setup, a large mirror with lights placed on both sides will be fine.

See page 173 for basic supplies that you'll need to complete a range of makeup styles. You can find most of them in some form at the makeup counter of your local drugstore. (You may have some in your home already, but ask before you raid the medicine cabinet!) You'll need to go to a costume-supply shop for greasepaint, facial hairpieces, spirit gum, warts, fake blood, nose putty, spray-on hair color, etc.

## SILVER THREADS AMONG THE GOLD: GOING GRAY WITHOUT GETTING OLDER

Okay, you've got to go gray—fast. Gray hair sprays are one solution, though they tend to get gloppy and look unnatural, making your head look like it's covered with cake frosting instead of hair. Wigs are another. The good ones are expensive; the cheap ones tend to look like mops, small furry creatures, or dirty rugs. A great alternative is to use a bit of white clown greasepaint, which you apply with an old toothbrush.

Dip the bristles into the makeup and, starting at your temples, brush it into your hair. Don't overload the toothbrush or attempt to cover every single hair. The trick is to use a light hand and work in the white gradually. Take a look at folks who are going gray, and you'll notice that the temples and front hairline tend to go gray first. If you apply too much, remove the excess with a tissue or run another old toothbrush over the excessive areas.

A quick shampoo will restore your locks to their youthful luster.

*Left, Rebecca Romijn-Stamos undergoes a transformation for* X-Men *(2000).*

# Masks

You've seen the masks of comedy and tragedy. These two faces, one grinning madly, the other terribly sad, symbolize Theater with a capital T. Ever wonder why? Masks, both real and imaginary, have always been part of Eastern and Western theater. In ancient Greek productions (we're talking sixth century B.C.E.) an actor wouldn't think of stepping onstage without a mask, which was very large and made of linen, wood, or leather. The mask's exaggerated features powerfully telegraphed the character's gender, age, and emotions, often to a huge gathering of viewers. Some historians used to think that the mask functioned as a kind of megaphone, helping to project the actor's voice. Microphones were several centuries away.

There was a practical side to the masks as well. A change of mask and costume would quickly transform the actor into an entirely new character, allowing him—and for centuries, all actors were boys or men—to play several roles in a single production.

Japanese No drama, which began in the fourteenth century and is still performed today, uses more than one hundred masks. Each is created to represent a certain type—gods, goddesses, goblins, devils, old people, and so on—and is made of wood and plaster, lacquered and beautifully gilded. Other traditional Asian theater forms, like those of Tibet, China, and Bali, use masks made of many different materials, including papier-mâché, wood, copper, horsehair, feathers, and cloth.

In sixteenth-century Italy, commedia dell'arte was born. Though the words translate as "comedy of art," the term itself came to mean "theater of the professionals." The masks used in these improvised comedies were designed to portray stock characters and were usually made of leather. Some concealed the actor's entire face; others ended just beneath the nose (and what an outrageous nose it was!) or covered only the eyes, which of course revealed the identity of the performer.

These days, other than at Mardi Gras or Halloween, we see masks only occasionally. This may be changing, thanks in part to the artist Julie Taymor, whose fantastic masks for Broadway's *The Lion King* and *The Green Bird* give us a taste of their amazing theatrical power. If you want to make your own mask, here is a plan for a neutral mask. You can use it for the exercises on page 41.

## Make a Neutral Mask

Here's what you need:
• a few sheets of tracing or copy paper
• a sheet or two of 8½" × 11" lightweight black, white, or brown cardboard (grab a couple of extras in case of mistakes)
• enough elastic to stretch comfortably from one temple to the other around the back of your head
• a pencil
• a stapler
• scissors or a craft knife
(If you want to use the knife, you must first get permission from a grown-up and use it only on a protected surface.)

This template will get you started. Take it to a copy shop and have it enlarged 150 percent. Then trace it onto a thin sheet of paper. This way, you'll have a pattern that you can make slightly larger or smaller if you need to. Plus, you won't have to cut up this book (!). Before you cut the holes for the eyes and nose, check to be sure they are in the right place for your own features. You will probably have to make a few adjustments: not everyone's eyes and nose are positioned in

exactly the same place between the top of the head and the chin. DON'T poke the holes while holding the template in front of your face! Instead, make a light pencil mark on the paper where it rests over your eyes and nostrils, then remove it to do the cutting.

Once you have the right size paper template, trace it onto the cardboard and cut it out.

Check once more to be certain that it fits. Next, staple the ends of the elastic that you have measured before cutting onto the inside of the mask at eye level and, to avoid a possible scratch, put pieces of adhesive tape over the staples on the side that touches your face. Happy miming!

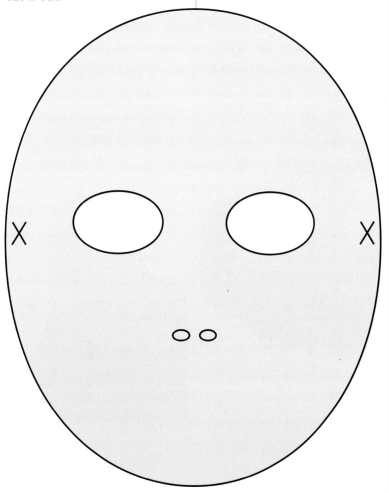

# Hey, Baldie!

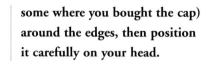

After a quick trip to the costume-supply shop, you, too, can be bald! Almost all baldcaps come with clear instructions, but just in case, here are the basics for creating a believable dome:

• Make sure that you buy the right size baldcap. If it's too large it will look like a weirdly wrinkled flesh-colored hat. If it's too tight, your hair will stick out in a fringe all around.

• Before you put the cap on, brush your hair off your face and up off your neck. Hold it in place with hair spray. You will need a fair amount.

Now follow these steps:

1. Carefully pull the cap over your scalp. You'll probably have to trim the cap so that it fits properly around your ears. Have someone else do this to avoid an accidental nick. Tuck in any stray hairs.

2. Apply the adhesive that comes with the cap (if it doesn't, be sure to ask for

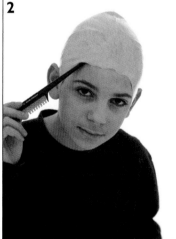

some where you bought the cap) around the edges, then position it carefully on your head.

3. Run your fingers along the edge to smooth the ridges. You want the cap to blend as much as possible with your own skin. Wipe away any adhesive that seeps out from underneath the rim.

Note: You may want to apply some foundation along the rim to hide where the cap ends and you begin.

Voilà! Now it's time to give your mom or dad a fright.

## Makeup

**1. Foundation:** a flesh-toned base coat that you apply to your face, neck, ears, and any other exposed skin with a sponge or your fingers. It comes in a dry cake form that you wet before applying, in a cream, or in a liquid. You may need to blend a few different shades to achieve the look or color that you want.

**2. Shadow:** a powder, stick, or cream used to define or change the shape of and highlight your features. Want to make your nose narrower? Apply a dark shadow to the sides, from the top of the nostrils to where the cartilage stops, and a thin band of highlight shadow down the center of your nose.

**3. Eyebrow pencil:** a stick used to define, extend, or change the shape of your brows. You can also use it to give yourself freckles.

**4. Eyeliner:** a liquid, brush, or stick used to line your eyelids or create a stylized look, à la Cleopatra.

**5. Mascara:** black or dark brown to define your lashes and open up your eyes.

**6. Rouge:** a powder, stick, or cream that can be used to give your cheeks a rosy glow and help define your cheekbones. If it's in stick or cream form, you can use it to give your lips color (you can also use a lip pencil or lipstick).

**7. Powder:** used to "set" your makeup so it won't smear or melt while you're performing and perspiring under hot lights. Apply it with a big powder brush or a puff. Blot gently or all of your meticulous makeup work will be rubbed off.

*Jar Jar Binks in* Star Wars Episode I: The Phantom Menace *(1999)*

*Check out the cool SFX makeup used on Darth Maul in* Star Wars Episode I: The Phantom Menace *(1999).*

**8. Makeup Remover:** when the show is over, you need to take it all off. Makeup removers are designed to lift the makeup off your skin gently and efficiently. There are many varieties of removers on the market: creams, oils, liquids. Whichever you choose, never scrub.

## Makeup Supplies

- Tissues for blotting and runny noses
- Makeup remover pads or cotton balls
- A small hand mirror for close work; if one side is magnified, all the better for applying those lashes and blemishes
- Cosmetic sponges for applying foundation and blending
- Makeup brushes: a few small ones designed for eye and lip lining, a medium-size one for eye and highlight shadowing, and a large poofy one for powder

# chapter nine

# Screen Test

*Panning, Zooming, Montage & Other Techniques • Gesture & Delivery •*
*Screenplays • Close-up, Over-the-Shoulder & Other Shots •*
*Buzz Tracks, Fades, Jump Cuts • Television*

Quiet on the set! Three, two, one, action! So you want to be in pictures, do you? Think of it: your name in lights, your image thirty feet tall on the silver screen. All that glamour and celebrity. "Please, no autographs just now, I'm off to meet with my personal trainer." Yipes!

Before you let your fantasies get the better of you, you might want to know that working in front of the camera—like every other aspect of acting, from basic warm-ups to final dress rehearsals—requires skill, concentration, and patience. Not only do you need to know your lines and understand your character; you need to understand how to shape your performance for the camera's all-seeing lens.

*Judy Garland's Dorothy clicks her ruby slippers together in* The Wizard of Oz *(1939).*

Guided by the director and DP (director of photography), the camera acts like a pair of eyes—one big cyclops eye, actually—choosing what the audience will see. It can **pan** the action on a busy city street, **cut** to the happy chaos of a family dinner, and **zoom in** for an intimate close-up on a laughing baby. So what's your role in all of this panning, cutting, and zooming? Making sure you're in the right place at the right time—if you're **out of frame,** you're out of luck—and understanding your character so well that you can snap into focus at a moment's notice. (For definitions of these terms, see Movie Lingo, pages 185–188.)

# Stage vs. Camera

But first, before diving into the nitty-gritty of performing for the camera, it's helpful to recognize some basic differences between the stage and screen. Even when equipped with gadgets that make it turn, tilt, and open up, the stage itself stays put in the theater, park, or auditorium where it happens to be. Any journeys that take place happen in the audience's imagination. And, depending on the size of the house—the part of the theater where the audience sits—someone sitting in row A will see details like eye color, trimming on a costume, even subtle changes in expression that someone sitting way back in Row Z will miss. This is why actors train to project their actions and emotions to the very last seat. As you know, this doesn't mean they flail their arms and shout at the top of their lungs, but that they direct their performance out to the audience.

*George Lucas (left) and Steven Spielberg (right) collaborated on* Raiders of the Lost Ark *(1981).*

Film, on the other hand, is a totally portable medium that can go just about anywhere: underwater, underground, even into space, depending on the story and the budget. Whether stuck way up front in Row A or happily chomping popcorn in Row Z, the entire audience participates in basically the same virtual ride.

Because the action on a stage is live, taking place in real time, exciting mistakes as well as dazzling performances can happen. Lines might be flubbed and brilliantly recovered. Props might be misplaced. An understudy may get a sudden, stunning break. There's a wealth of possibilities!

The actors in a film don't enter and exit a scene as they do on a stage. They don't even perform before an audience, unless you count the director, producers, and crew. And, unlike actors performing live theater, who keep going no matter what, film actors' performances are constantly being interrupted. If a plane suddenly flies overhead, interfering with the sound recording, Cut! If a light is out of place, Cut! If an actor is even slightly out of frame, Cut! You need to know your own acting process well enough that the stop-and-start nature of film doesn't throw off your concentration and, eventually, your performance. For some people this means being quiet and not talking to others. For others it means finding a quiet corner to run through a series of physical exercises. You have to honor your process, whatever it is. Concentration is like a muscle. You have to exercise it for it to work well.

In addition to stopping and starting, there are other potential distractions: hot lights; the weather; long, unpredictable workdays (one day you work six hours, the next you wait around all day and end up working just ten minutes); and shooting **out of sequence.** If you act in a film, you might

**David** *Acting in movies and TV is a little bit easier than acting onstage. When you're acting onstage, it's every night, and it's live. If you mess up, you can't just say "Cut" and do it over. You have to keep alert. It's fun because it will be different each time. And you hear the audience's applause.*

**Sophie** *You have to be aware of where the camera is at every moment and listen carefully to the director's instructions. You don't want the cameraperson to have to do an extra take because you weren't paying attention.*

*Sir Alec Guinness (Obi-Wan Kenobi) and director George Lucas on the set of* Star Wars *(1977).*

## FOOD! WATER!

**I**n movies and television, young people have legal time limits on the set and are supposed to have a parent or guardian present. There are also firm laws about time away from school, breaks, and being fed: they're not allowed to deny you an education, have you work four hours straight, or starve you.

very well shoot the ending scene on the first day, come back the next for the opening, and return on the third for a few more takes on the end. There's lots of "hurry up and wait." This isn't disorganization or a desire on the part of the production people to confuse the cast; it has to do with what's the most efficient and economical **shooting schedule.**

It's helpful to remind yourself that the director wants you to do well and, ideally, will create an atmosphere on the set that is conducive to creating the best film possible. You'll be happiest if you stay open to the overall vision of the film and try not to get a rigid idea of your character. Be responsive to direction and criticism. No matter how well you think you know your character or the motivations behind his or her actions, the director knows the film. You can't know during its making what the final outcome will be. You have to trust the director and be willing to let go of some of the control that you have onstage.

Once the actors' on-camera work is done, long before the

premiere, it is then integrated into the story through an intricate collage of visuals, color, music, and sound that comes together in the editing room. During the editing phase the film is shaped into a coherent whole. Bits of **footage** will be moved around and put into proper order and, depending on the artistic and practical needs of the director, editor, and producers, entire scenes—and possibly a few fabulous performances—may end up on the cutting-room floor. An actor may be called into a sound studio to "dub" (do voice-overs) his or her lines if they weren't clear. Ambient noises like the sound of heels clicking on pavement or traffic outside a living room window may be enhanced or removed, and a musical score and titles and credits will be created and added. This complicated process is similar to assembling a great jigsaw puzzle, which reveals its image piece by piece.

# The Impact of Gesture and Delivery

Film's ability to get up close and personal reveals the smallest details we notice in the course of daily life. For example, if someone looks away when you greet him or doesn't shake your hand warmly, it comes across strongly on film. The camera seems to actually magnify actions and expressions. The flicker of an eyelash can have major emotional impact. This intimacy demands an extremely subtle form of communication from the actors. This doesn't mean mumbling. It means understanding how to pull back slightly to allow the closeness of the camera to capture every nuance. You have to be clear about what those nuances are about. If you are

**Jen** *In theater, you get to work up to big emotional moments. In film and TV you might have no preparation and things are shot out of sequence. It's "today we're doing your death, and tomorrow we're doing your birthday party." They each require totally different acting techniques. It's difficult getting used to a camera standing in for a person, and to the crew standing around eating sandwiches while you're supposed to be having an intimate conversation. In theater, everything has to be bigger, so you can reach the audience. You have to scale back your performance for the camera.*

supposed to be sad, why exactly? Maybe you have to eat your broccoli, or maybe something truly terrible has happened. Every emotion creates a different expression on your face.

Just like stage directors, some film directors are very specific about every move you make and where you direct your gaze. Others give you a wide latitude. Your job is to learn as much as you can about the medium itself: how the camera moves, which kinds of shots are being used. The more you know, the more comfortable you will be in front of the

*Joe Flaherty (left) and Eugene Levy (right) of* Second City Television *mug for the camera.*

camera. You have to ask a lot of questions. Is it a close-up? Will the camera be in your face or will the DP use a zoom? How wide is the shot? The camera has a long lens. Even if it's placed far away from you, the shot may be a zoom that includes just your chin to your forehead. The smallest motion of your mouth will be huge. You have to stay super-aware of your subconscious and learn how to control some habitual expressions. The fact that your eyebrows go up and down a lot when you speak might go unnoticed in the course of normal conversation or onstage yet read as an impossible-to-ignore nervous twitch when projected fifteen feet tall. "Wow, that guy's brows never stop wiggling!"

# Become a Film Buff

The best way to learn about film is to watch lots of movies. You must have at least a few favorites. Rent one that you especially like and study it carefully. Since you already know the story, you can devote your attention to how the director has shaped the film and each character's place within that shape. Do the actors come across as "real" people or are they shot with lots of elaborate lighting and makeup? Do they maintain their characterizations from scene to scene or are there inconsistencies in behavior or use of mannerisms? What kinds of shots are used? Does the camera jump around like in a music video or are its movements seamless and smooth? How do the camera's motions affect the storytelling or mood? What do you think of the sound track? Is the music integrated smoothly or does it seem to be tacked on as an afterthought? Now that you are becoming aware of all the pieces that go into creating the film puzzle, you probably have ideas about what you would you do differently if you were the director.

*Keanu Reeves in* The Matrix *(1999)*

# Screenplays

Analyzing a screenplay is similar to analyzing a play script (see page 105). It's important to be able to track your character's development at any given moment. You want to follow his or her journey through the story and be able to identify specific turning points. Because films are almost always shot out of sequence, you also want to be clear about

# Movie Faves

Here's a totally random list of favorite movies from a small sampling of opinionated kids and grown-ups. You'll add a bunch of your own, and probably subtract a few in the process.

★ *Funniest*

*Ace Ventura, Pet Detective* (1994)

*Duck Soup* (Marx Brothers, 1933)

*Dumb and Dumber* (1994)

*High Anxiety* (1977)

*The Man with Two Brains* (1983)

*Modern Times* (Charlie Chaplin, 1936)

*The Nutty Professor* (1996)

*The Pink Panther* movies (all of them)

*Sherlock, Jr.* (Buster Keaton, 1924)

*Take the Money and Run* (1969)

*Young Frankenstein* (1974)

★ *Best Dramas*

*All Quiet on the Western Front* (1930)

*Beauty and the Beast* (1946 version)

*The Bicycle Thief* (1948)

*Citizen Kane* (1941)

*Ever After: A Cinderella Story* (1998)

*The Grapes of Wrath* (1940)

*On the Waterfront* (1954)

*One Flew over the Cuckoo's Nest* (1975)

*Rain Man* (1988)

*Rebel Without a Cause* (1955)

*Sense and Sensibility* (1995)

*James Dean in* Rebel Without a Cause

★ *Best Visual Effects (VFX) and/or Sound Effects (SFX)*

*Alien* (1992)

*The Animal* (2001)

*Batman* movies

*Close Encounters of the Third Kind* (1977)

*Crouching Tiger, Hidden Dragon* (2000)

*Dr. Seuss' How the Grinch Stole Christmas* (2000)

*The 5,000 Fingers of Dr. T.* (Dr. Seuss, 1952)

*Gladiator* (2000)

*The Matrix* (1999)

*Men in Black* (1997)

*Mission Impossible II* (2000)

*The Mummy Returns* (2001)

*The Perfect Storm* (1999)

*Planet of the Apes* (2001)

*Star Wars* trilogy

*Titanic* (1997)

*2001: A Space Odyssey* (1968)

*X-Men* (2000)

★ *Best Costumes: Most Outrageous, Most Beautiful, Etc.*

*Amadeus* (1984)

*Braveheart* (1995)

*Crouching Tiger, Hidden Dragon* (2000)

*Dr. Seuss' How the Grinch Stole Christmas* (2000)

*Dune* (1984)

*Excalibur* (1981)

*Funny Face* (1957)

*Gandhi* (1982)

*Henry V* (1989)

*Jurassic Park* (1993)

*The Last Emperor* (1987)

*Little Women* (1994)

*Metropolis* (1926)

*Pee Wee's Big Adventure* (1985)

*Road Warrior* movies

*Star Trek* movies

*Star Wars* trilogy

*The Wizard of Oz* (1939)

what happened just before a particular scene, and just after. If you're on top of your character's actions and emotions at every moment, as well as his or her place in the overall story, you will find it much easier to tap into the proper emotions and deliver a strong performance when a scene is thrown at you out of the blue—which it certainly will be. ("My graduation scene? But I haven't done the orientation scene yet!")

# Camera Work

It's helpful to know what kind of shot is being done. If you understand what the camera is doing in a particular scene, you can shape your performance accordingly. "I'm ready for my close-up!" Okay. You had better be.

A **close-up** (see photo at right) reveals details like the flowers on a blooming plant, the brick pattern on a building, or subtle changes of facial expression. It conveys intimacy by showing a character's emotional reactions. Since the camera doesn't actually have to be physically close to the subject for a close-up shot (the cameraperson can zoom in from a position way across the room), it's important to know what, exactly, will be in the frame. It might be your head and shoulders or perhaps only your hands fidgeting in your lap. An extreme close-up comes in even tighter, capturing just your eyes or maybe a tiny insect working its way across a blade of grass.

A **medium** shot (see photo at right) shows a broader view of a scene than a close-up does. It might capture you from the waist up or

focus on a chair and a table in the corner of a room. It's often used to capture a conversation between two characters. A **wide** shot (also known as an **establishing shot** or long shot; see photo, top left) can be used to "establish" or "set" a scene or to capture a lot of movement, like a bustling classroom packed with active kindergartners.

An **over-the-shoulder** (see photo, bottom left) shot may be used if the camera is tracking an intimate conversation between you and another actor. The camera is positioned over your shoulder to create the impression that you are looking directly at the person you are talking to. It's used in interior car scenes a lot, to capture a conversation between characters riding in the front seat and those sitting in the back. A **cutaway** shot can be a kind of detour from the main action, cutting away from your intimate conversation to capture a third person entering the room. These two shots are often used as transitions between scenes.

All of this shifting and zooming can be disorienting for actors. It can seem as if the film is nothing more than dozens

and dozens of isolated "takes" that just don't connect. You need to trust the director and cinematographer and allow yourself to be placed within that puzzle and understand that even if something feels awkward or they seem to be after a detail that strikes you as unimportant, there's usually a reason that will become clear later. For more Movie Lingo, see pages 185–188.

# The Small Screen

A TV shoot can be much quicker and more high-pressured than a film shoot. It might take just one day. A much tighter shooting schedule means that there's a lot less room for mistakes. There are other differences, too. The television is a small screen, as opposed to the large screen for films. Your performance plays differently. You're relatively tiny instead of huge, for one thing. Also, a movie audience makes the effort to come and see you. And they pay money for their tickets. Not so with television. You are in someone's living room. And you can be gone with a flick of the remote, without a second thought on the part of the person surfing the channels. If you get a part on a soap opera—a "soap" to those in the biz—or a sitcom (situation comedy), be happy! It can be a great way to launch a career. Meg Ryan, Ellen Barkin, Demi Moore, and Ricky Martin are among the many performers who got their starts in soaps. Your work on a soap may take place over several days. Those days may be close together, if you're lucky, or spread out over many months. If this is the case, you'll (hopefully) have other jobs in between and have to work extra hard to keep your characterization strong. You don't want to seem out of touch.

**Joey** *TV is more challenging than theater because in theater you can always do a better performance next time. With TV you have to do it right or you end up doing a take over and over, a million times. Your performance should not be as big as in a theater because you don't have to project as far.*

# Movie Lingo

Just like the theater, the movies have a techie vocabulary all their own. Master a few of the terms here, and you'll be on your way to becoming a PA (production assistant).

**Buzz track.** This is a mostly silent stretch of sound that is recorded for "atmosphere." The sound person will ask

**David**  *When you act for the screen, you do exactly what the director tells you to do. The stage is freer. You can ad-lib a bit. For example, if the director tells you to "walk over there," you might be able to choose how you walk. You put more of your own thoughts into what you do. Film doesn't have as much of that. When you're in front of the camera, you see the mike, lights, reflectors, and everything. You have to ignore all that to do your scene. It's a lot less realistic. You have to not look at the camera, unless they tell you to. Personally, I don't know which I like better. I like them both.*

everyone on the set to be absolutely quiet for about a minute while he or she records what is called "ambient" sound: sounds in the background that you might not be aware of—until they're not there. If you're in a city park, for example, there might be the sound of cars driving by, leaves rustling in the trees, or children shouting and laughing. An **interior** (inside) scene might have the sound of a radiator gurgling or a fan humming. Often actors are called back in after a movie has finished shooting to rerecord their dialogue over the buzz track to create a more natural scene.

**Close-up.** A shot that zeros in on a small part of the subject or scene. Close-ups are wonderful for revealing essential detail and emotions.

**Cut.** This term has several meanings: a cut is a strip of film that contains a single shot. (A "shot" is what a take is called after it's edited.) A cut is also the linking of two shots during editing as well as the separation of one shot from another—like when a director cuts from a shot of the kitchen table to a shot of the boy eating cereal on the floor. And, of course, a director calls out, "Cut!" when he or she wants the cameraperson to stop shooting.

**Day for night.** This wonderful term describes the process of shooting nighttime scenes during the daytime. This is done a number of ways, including adding a blue filter to the camera lens and underexposing the shot. If you've ever taken an underexposed photograph, you know how dark the image looks. Another technique is to shoot at what's called the "magic hour," just after the sun goes down, when the sky is dark blue instead of the black of night. Streetlights or specially arranged film lights add just the right amount of illumination.

**Dissolve.** A dramatic transition device that involves superimposing one image over another. As the new image comes into focus, the one underneath dissolves.

**Establishing shot.** Just what it sounds like: a shot to establish the setting. It's often the first shot of a scene.

**Fade-in/fade-out.** Unlike a dissolve, which is used to connect scenes, fade-ins and fade-outs are used to separate scenes by moving from a blank screen to a picture (fade-in), or fading from a picture to a black or white screen (fade-out).

**Footage.** What film is called after it has been shot. James Cameron, director of *Titanic,* shot 1.3 million feet of footage. That adds up to more than 4,333 football fields!

**Jump cut.** An abrupt cut from one scene to another. It could be cutting from a man lounging in the bathtub to a shot of kids on a Ferris wheel in an amusement park. Jump cuts are used to call attention to something or to surprise the audience. Music videos are packed with jump cuts.

**Live area.** The area of the film that will actually be viewed. The camera records a larger area than what will be seen once the film is edited. The area beyond the live area is called the "safe area."

**Montage.** The word means "assemblage" in French. In film language, it is a valuable story device consisting of a sequence of often unrelated shots that are connected by dissolves. A montage usually has no dialogue; music is often added to enhance a sense of time passing or intense emotions.

**On location.** If you're shooting on location, you're shooting in a place that already exists. It might be the actual place it is supposed to be, like Grand Central Terminal, for example, or a location that looks close enough to the real thing to "fool" the audience.

**Optical.** You've heard of a "dissolve" or a "fade." These are opticals: special-effect visual techniques that are often used to create a sense of time passing and to connect or separate scenes. They can happen in the camera itself or in **post-production,** when the film is being edited.

**Out of frame.** Anything out of frame is beyond the range of what the camera is recording.

**Pan.** A side-to-side movement of the camera. A panning shot can be used to follow someone or something moving, show off a landscape, or turn the audience's attention to something new.

**Shooting schedule.** A timeline detailing when and where each shot will be filmed.

**Video assist.** Sometimes called a "video tap," it transfers footage the director is shooting to a video monitor so it can be checked as it's being shot.

**Zoom.** When the camera moves in close (zoom in) or pulls away (zoom out) from its subject. The camera itself can stay put during a zoom, with all the action happening through adjustments to the lens.

# chapter ten

# Making a Living

*Headshots • Agents • Casting Directors • Auditioning • Casting •
Commercials • Voice-overs • Print Work • Industrials • Unions*

If you want to try to make a professional "go" of it, there are many ways to approach a career in acting. First you need to let the world know you're ready. This doesn't mean standing on a rooftop and shouting, "I'm ready, world!" It means getting your business act together—the part of you that meets and greets the world on paper as well as in person.

**The Big Picture**

If you want to go pro, you should . . .

★ Always ask for feedback

★ Don't take rejection personally

★ Cultivate professional friendships and relationships

★ Keep your headshots and résumé up to date

★ Be positive and realistic

★ Keep exploring your craft

★ Have fun

# Headshots

Photographs of yourself (a.k.a. **headshots**) are necessary if you plan to go to more than a few auditions. Along with your résumé (see page 191), they are your calling card. If your headshots are sent out in advance of an audition by an agent or casting director (page 192), they give those holding the audition an opportunity to see if you're the right "type" for a particular part, and to decide if they want you to come in for an interview or reading. If you bring them with you to an audition, they're a handy way for those holding the audition to remember you.

The photos should show you being you. This means no heavy makeup, outlandish hairstyles, clunky jewelry, weird clothing (leave the vampire cape in your closet), pets, or random brothers or sisters. Your face and torso should fill up most of the picture. Traditional headshots—photos taken from the chest up—never go out of style. Your mom or dad, a relative, or a family friend can take your pictures. There is no reason to go running off to a photo studio. Because you are still growing and changing, you'll need to have another set done in nine months or so, anyway. (By then you might have your braces off!) If and when you go the agent route (see page 192), you may be asked to pose for a set shot by a professional photographer.

It's a good idea to shoot the photos outside, in daylight. Look directly into the camera—good practice for the big time—and smile naturally. Smile with your entire face. When people smile with their mouths and not their eyes, the effect is downright creepy. Try some different poses. If you're thinking that you might audition for commercials, you'll want to take some pictures wearing an accessory like a baseball hat and an extra-big smile. Be sure to look at the camera. Profile shots may be arty, but they're of no use to casting directors. When you have several that you like, whittle your selections down to two favorites that show different aspects of your personality. Maybe in one you have a broad, open smile and in the other you appear more pensive or soulful. Choose with care. You're trying to reveal as much of your personality and your "look" as you can in just a few photos.

**Joey** *If you really want to pursue acting, get headshots. Black-and-white, definitely, with a little bit of attitude.*

# Résumés

Every actor who goes out for jobs needs an up-to-date résumé. It's a quick way for a director or casting agent to learn something about you. It has to be typed and free of spelling errors. A hand-scrawled sheet torn out of a notebook just won't cut it. Keep the information basic: your name, numbers where you can be contacted, your height, weight, hair and eye color, age range—you might be a twelve-year-old who can play kids up to fourteen or as young as nine—and, if you sing, your vocal range. If you have had any theater, film, or television experience, including commercials, list that next. If you've done a commercial, you'll indicate that you have a videotape, "available upon request" (see Commercials, page 202). Include the training you've had, and any special skills that you possess. **Don't undersell yourself, and don't embellish.** Honesty is always, always

the best policy. If you know how to ride a horse or play the violin, exercise those bragging rights! But don't pretend you have more experience or skills than you do. If you can't do handsprings or speak Portuguese, don't list them among your accomplishments. Of course, if you're confident that you can learn a particular skill in time, go for it.

# Agents and Casting Directors

Agents and casting directors are professionals who have connections to directors and producers. Their job is to find actors to fill roles in film, theater, television, and commercials. A casting director is a scout who keeps track of many actors and, when a film or theater director needs to fill a particular role, will audition those who he or she thinks are possible for the part. Actors who make the "first cut"—who look and act right and have the right kind of experience—are invited to return for a "callback," which is a second audition in front of the director and possibly the producers and other members of the production team. (See The Audition's Over, Now What?, page 201.)

Interviewing and signing with an agent is a big step, and a highly individual one. If you are getting serious about acting and want to have the opportunity to audition for parts that might not be listed in local newspapers or posted on your school or community bulletin boards, you might want to think about getting an agent. Like a casting director, an agent keeps track of lots of actors and, ideally, stays on top of the latest shows, films, and commercials. He or she should also be

**Joey** *I got an agent right away because my older sister had one, and she liked me. An agent can help you get into certain auditions.*

plugged in to the audition network, and have connections to directors, producers, and casting directors. One big difference is that if an agent chooses to represent you—and you feel comfortable being the agent's client—the two of you will sign a contract. Agents represent only actors whom they feel warrant an investment of their time. If and when you do sign with an agent, you should expect that your photos and résumé will be sent to directors and casting agents looking for a certain type (your type!) of actor. Your agent might also help you compose and update your résumé and advise you as to what classes you might take and what sorts of headshots you should have, sometimes recommending a professional photographer. He or she may take an active role in shaping your career, like recommending what kinds of parts you should, or shouldn't, go after. If an audition your agent sends you to results in an acting job, the agent then takes a percentage (usually 10–15 percent) of your fee. You should *never* pay an agent before you get a job.

If you want to go the casting director and/or agent route, it's important to ask around to find out who the best people are. Actors who have work are a great resource. The **best people are also the busiest,** which means that you have to be patient and approach them through the proper channels, which is usually through the mail. In addition to your résumé and photos, you should include a short cover letter explaining who you are, what you've done, information about any show you're lucky enough to have been a part of, who referred you (if someone did), and that you would like to come in for an interview and will give a call in a week or so. When you call, you may or may not be asked to come in. If you are, great! You have a foot in the door. If not, don't despair. Simply ask when might be a good time to call again.

★ **David** *I started when I was nine years old. I loved to sing, so my mom said I should get some training. My singing teacher said I should act, too, and recommended me to an acting coach, who taught me the basics and said, You can act and sing, why don't you audition for an agent who needs some new talent? After I got my agent, it took me a while to get my first job, a musical. But I wasn't disappointed. I expected it to take time. Agents will find what you're good for. If they want a sweet soprano choirboy with blond hair and blue eyes, they wouldn't send me there, because I'm nothing like that. Agents can get you into more auditions that you're better for, and into some that you can't go to unless you have an agent or manager.*

In the meantime, put the agent at the top of your mailing list (after Grandma and Grandpa, of course) so you'll be sure to send notices of any acting work you're doing. And, of course, also try someone else.

# Promo

Part of your job as an actor is to promote yourself. Does this mean standing on a street corner and yelling, "I'm the greatest thing since sliced bread, hire me!" Of course not. It means staying in touch with casting directors and agents and keeping them up to the minute with your relevant activities. (But they don't need to know about your new dog, cute though he may be.) Once you've sent your photos, résumé, and cover letter, you can jog their memories every couple of months with a "reminder," maybe a postcard that features your photo. You can have a bunch made up for relatively little money. This gives them another look at you and a quick rundown of what you're up to. **Be sure your photo reflects your current age and look,** and don't forget to include your name and the all-important contact numbers.

At some point you may feel like you're not getting anywhere. You've been making follow-up calls and sending out cards for months and haven't had a single response. Never fear! Acting is a fickle and mysterious business. Maybe you need to expand your list of agents and casting directors. It could be the people you've been showering with your images and info don't handle your type and are too busy to let you know.

So what type are you? The truth is that though nobody is simply a "type"—we're all too complex to be defined just by the way we look—directors in a hurry, as they almost always seem to be, need a shorthand way to describe the sort of actor they are looking for. Once you're in front of them—if you're fortunate enough to fit the description!—they'll appreciate all of the other stuff that goes into who you are.

A good way to begin to define your type is to look at lots of actors and the kinds of roles they play. You'll see that certain body types and facial features tend to correspond to certain roles: the angry young man, the bubbly teenage girl, the annoying little brother . . . At some point you may want a part badly enough to go for it even if you are totally "wrong." Let's say it calls for a bubbly teenage girl and you're a somber eleven-year-old who at first glance projects bookworm instead of bubbles. You might be lucky. You may wow them with your talent, and there may be some flexibility in terms of the "look." This is known as **casting against type.**

Above all, you must continue to study your craft. A happy actor is one who enjoys the process, not simply the rewards. As you grow and develop, you'll find new ways to approach your career.

★ **Jen** *I did* Knee-high to a Microphone *at Centerstage Theater in New York City. I was part of a cast of sixteen. We wrote it and all acted in it. It's a collection of monologues, scenes, and songs that aren't connected to each other but relate to the topics of prejudice against teens and teens finding their own voice. It had a two-week run. Centerstage has two resident companies: Labyrinth, which is getting lots of attention because of the actor Philip Seymour Hoffman, and Developing Artists, for younger performers, ages thirteen to twenty.*

★ **Patrick** *I've been in* Les Misérables *on Broadway. I was Gavroche, a street urchin. I was Tiny Tim in* A Christmas Carol *at Madison Square Garden. And I was Chip the Teacup on a national tour of* Beauty and the Beast *for two years.*

> ★ **Jen** *A lot of times it's frustrating when the people around you start making it, like getting parts on TV series, and you feel like you're going nowhere. There are a lot of times, especially when your friends are the same type as you are, when there can be competition and jealousy. I believe that my time will come. I have patience and perspective. I'm not out there looking for fame and fortune. I'm happy to keep working and find interesting characters to work on.*

> ★ **Joey** *Never say, "I can't." That will lower your confidence, and you'll be bad! And you need to keep socializing.*

> ★ **Jen** *Without a doubt, take lots of classes. Always go to auditions, even if it doesn't seem that you'll be totally right for the part. Every time you do it, you'll get a little bit better. And get out there and act, anytime you can, in community theater or at school. It all adds up.*

# Building Experience

Since the chances of being discovered by a famous director while sipping a soda at the local drugstore are pretty slim (ask your grandparents to tell you how Lana Turner was discovered doing just that), you'll probably have to build your acting résumé step by step. Every acting experience, no matter how small, teaches you something valuable. Don't be in a mad rush. The point is to get started. You might begin with a school play or a role in a community theater—situations where you don't need an agent or a casting director to get you an audition.

If you're studying acting, your school is a great resource. You may be invited to participate in a classroom production, and you'll certainly hear about auditions. Always check the bulletin board for notices. **Make a point of attending as many productions around town as you can and sticking around afterward to talk to members of the cast and crew.** You might learn about an audition or classes. If you really like the company's work, it's worth getting involved any way you can. You might try behind-the-scenes work, as a member of the costume, stagehand, or lighting crew—a valuable opportunity to learn about theater from the inside. And if you're offered a part, take it. Keep an open mind, and each and every experience will teach you something new—about the theater and about yourself.

Realistically, **it may be several years before you start to get the roles that you think you deserve.** There is no magic formula for success. Many actors never reach their initial career goals and find happiness only when they refocus their energies on different kinds of parts. One of the many wonderful things about acting is that you can do it your entire life, and in many different ways. Excellent roles exist, and are always being created, for actors who are young, old, or in between. You have to learn how to maintain perspective while continually refining your objectives and expanding your skills.

# Auditioning Skills

Every actor needs to learn how to audition. Some think of auditioning as foul-tasting medicine, an unpleasant but necessary step toward landing a part. This is too bad, considering that unless you become a huge star, and often even then, you will be going to auditions your entire career. If you're lucky! Other actors, more happily, think of each audition as a miniperformance and an opportunity to work on their acting skills. They get past the fact of being judged by imagining that those people sitting out there (judging them!) are a paying audience, eager to see the show that they're starring in. They also keep in mind that the requirements for a role may include things that they can't do anything about, like height, hair color, age range, or special skills. Or it may be as simple as the director's already having a particular actor in mind and just wanting to get a look at others to confirm his or her feelings.

No matter what the outcome, you want to keep auditioning. You may not land a part for what seems like ages, but every time you audition you will be improving your acting skills and growing more comfortable in front of an audience, and with the all-important business of being an actor. Always, always bring several copies of your photos and

**David**  *Don't think that because you went to twenty auditions and didn't get anything, you're a failure. You need to find the parts that fit who you are. You should try to get an agent who will do matchmaking. I have a manager who uses multiple agents and finds roles that I'm suited for. She gets calls and if she thinks I look right she will send over my picture and résumé.*

**Joey**  *Sometimes the casting people can be rude at auditions. Don't take it seriously. They've just had a long day.*

**Jen** *Auditioning used to be something I really hated, but now I see it as an opportunity to perform, especially if I get to do a monologue. Sonya's at the end of Chekhov's* Uncle Vanya *is just beautiful. Chekhov is so beautiful, difficult as well, so real and so natural. I start crying every time I hear it. It's so poetic that it gives me chills. To contrast that, I like anything from Christopher Durang. His* Laughing Wild *is a two-character play that is basically two monologues. I advise people to avoid Shakespeare at auditions, because even if you love it, there are lots of people who don't want to hear it. The language is so different.*

résumé along. The director or producer may very well ask you to leave a few; staple your résumé to the back of your photos. And don't forget your date book, in case you need to take down any information—or schedule a callback!

**Preparing for an Audition** If you are auditioning for a particular play, you'll want to get a copy from the library or bookstore and read it carefully in advance. If you know which role you will be going for, all the better. Study the part closely and make some decisions about how you want to play it. Imagine how the character looks, moves, and sounds. Determine whether she or he has a confident, open demeanor or one that is sad or timid, and if the character moves with ease or with awkward physical stress and strain. Decide if his or her voice is whispery and soft, loud and abrasive, or somewhere in between. You might want to consult your Character Journal (see page 73) for some ideas. No matter what you decide, you want to be sure that your character reflects the playwright's intentions as far as you know them. In other words, if the character is described as being a terrible bully, you'll want to come up with realistic supporting behavior. It's also valuable to try to learn as much about the production as possible. Any details as to how the director works and how he or she envisions the outcome will be helpful.

It's also essential to have a couple of contrasting monologues prepared: one funny and one serious, for example. Choose material that is appropriate to your age and gender and shows your range as a performer. (See Going It Alone [Monologues], page 84.) You might also, if you have a nice voice, prepare a song or two.

**Cold Readings** What if you aren't asked to perform a prepared monologue and don't have a chance to see the audition material ahead of time? You may walk into an audition and be handed a script that you've never laid eyes on. Clearly, you cannot whip up an instant portrait of a character you hardly know. So what do you do?

**1.** Ask to take a quick look at the script so you can get a sense of the part you'll be reading. You're going to have to make several courageous, split-second decisions about your character.

**2.** Don't fret about details. There's no time for nuance.

**3.** Ask yourself some questions: What are the character's motivations? What is he or she trying to do, and how?

**4.** Try, if you can, to imagine a bit of your character's inner life: any thoughts that may be contributing to behavior. Remember, there's no room here for particulars.

**5.** If you have the time, use these ideas to project a sense of your character's physicality (posture, walk, and gestures) and voice (quality and volume).

**David** *You never know what to expect. Every audition is different. But there are a few rules. You should always elaborate when they ask you a question. If they ask, "How are you?" don't just say, "Fine." Say, "Fine," then tell them about something that's happened recently. Otherwise, they'll think of you as shy. Always have a lot of energy. They don't care about how your day has gone. They just want to see your talent. At my first audition, I was nervous. I had practiced so many times, and I knew my material. Now it's like, "Hi, how are you doing?"*

Your goal here is to jump in with confidence and demonstrate your acting abilities. It's not about right or wrong. Even your rough sketch, because it's boldly drawn, will give those holding the audition a sense of your abilities.

**Staying Calm and Focused** Auditioning can jangle your nerves and disrupt your focus, there's no doubt about it. But there are ways to turn the jit-

**David** *I'm not going to sulk because I know that there will be other auditions and possibilities. You might not be the right look. I've been told that dozens of times. They might keep you in mind for something else.*

**Jen** *I'm really okay with it. It's part of the business. I go into an audition, then put it out of my mind. If they call me back, excellent. You can't take rejection personally. You may be the best person but too tall or don't fit the costume, or have the wrong color hair. There are so many stupid reasons. You have to have confidence in your acting.*

**Joey** *You have to give yourself time.*

ters to your advantage and make the experience a positive one. (See Stage Fright, page 109.) Give yourself ample time to prepare both physically and mentally. Be sure your date book and photos and résumé packets are packed in whichever bag you are carrying. Choose clothing that makes you feel comfortable and looks presentable. A torn sweatshirt and dirty jeans may feel just fine, but surely won't impress anyone. If you are going for a specific role and want to "dress the part," do so with care. Allow extra time to get to the audition—you can't control traffic jams, trains, or buses—and make every effort to arrive a few minutes ahead of your appointment. If your schedule is too scrunched and you're in a mad rush, you will feel stressed and worn out and it will be that much harder to stay calm and focused.

Okay, you've reached your destination and checked in.

**1.** Scope out the room, studio, or theater.

**2.** If there's a quiet corner, make a beeline for it. This is where you will warm up and collect your thoughts.

**3.** Run through whatever simple routine you have devised for auditions: probably some stretches, vocalizing (not too loud), and deep breathing. Obviously, it's not always possible or convenient to run through an entire series of exercises.

**4.** If there's no quiet corner to be found, try to shut out the noise and the crowd by closing your eyes for a moment and breathing. Deeply. Conjure up a relaxing image if you can.

**5.** Don't worry about the reactions of your classmates or fellow actors. If they're smart, they'll be doing their version of the same thing when it's time for them to perform.

**6.** Think about the material you will be performing, and remind yourself that auditions are an opportunity, not a curse! If this one doesn't yield a role, hey, there will be many more.

**7.** Try not to be distracted by the other waiting actors or by those who have finished and are on their way out the door.

**8.** Remind yourself of your name and how old you are. Believe it or not, it's not at all uncommon to forget these two crucial bits of information!

**9.** When it's time to actually audition, walk into the room and, depending on what's asked of you, give your photos and résumé to the director or producer, then find your mark. (Hint: don't walk in and talk at the same time.)

**10.** There will probably be a spot (a line or a T shape) on the floor marked with masking tape in front of whoever is holding the audition. This is where you will stand. So far, so good.

**11.** Introduce yourself and the monologue and/or song you will perform.

**12.** When you've finished, say thank you, answer any questions, and leave. Whatever happens, happens. You were prepared, stayed calm and focused, and did your best.

> ⭐ **Jen** *I've heard this over and over again, but it's so true. If you can find yourself even reasonably happy doing something else, do it. Acting is so hard and the business is so tough. Even SAG [Screen Actors Guild] is, like, 90 percent unemployment. There has to be nothing else that will make you happy. It's too much of a struggle and too much hardship otherwise. If you want fame and fortune, I'm sure there is an easier way to find it.*

# The Audition's Over, Now What?

You know how your parents are always nagging you to write thank-you notes for your birthday or holiday gifts? Well, now's the time to show off your good manners. **Send a note as soon as possible after your audition.** Keep it short and to the point. If you can think of something positive to say about the audition experience, all the better. Of course, you'll want to add the people you auditioned for to your mailing list. You may very well be invited to come in at some other point to try for another role or be given a callback for the role you auditioned for earlier. If you are given a callback, take advantage of the fact that you made an impression, and try to dress in the same clothing that you wore and perform similar, if not the same, material. They liked you enough the way you were to ask you back. You might be asked to read something new. View it as a chance to reveal more of your character and acting talent.

# Commercials

Whether you realize it or not, you're already a commercials expert. How so, you ask? Not only do you watch and listen to plenty of them on television and the radio, you concoct a bunch of your very own every single day: when you lobby your parents for a certain privilege, item of clothing, or extra allowance, when you lodge a complaint with your teacher or announce some startling new fact to your friends. Were they sold? If not, why not? Was it your tone of voice, your outrageous claim, or your less-than-passionate delivery? If you're interested in pursuing commercial work, it's a good idea to keep a running list of which ones you like and which irritate or bore you. How do the actors, whether they're on-camera or just a voice, come across? Are they believable? What makes them so? Do you like the sound track? What about the "look"—the setting, lighting, and camera work? Does it appeal to you or turn you off? What would you do differently if you had the opportunity? These exercises will help you zero in on the qualities that convince.

Many actors view commercial work as a good career stepping-stone. They get practical experience, learn to work at an extremely fast pace, and earn valuable professional credentials. If you do a commercial, you'll get a video- or audio-

tape that will prove useful because you can leave it at auditions and send it out—something else to remember you by!

There are some huge differences between commercials and what's known as "legitimate" theater, film, or television work. Not that commercial work isn't real work; actors who do commercials work very hard. Whether they're on-camera spots or **voice-overs**—jobs for television and radio where only the actor's voice is used—commercials demand a unique set of skills. They are about selling a product, service, or lifestyle, not about creating a character with a complex internal life. There isn't enough time, for one thing, since most run only about thirty seconds. The mood is almost always cheery and upbeat. Some actors may not feel comfortable with the selling aspect of commercials, and therefore may opt not to seek this kind of work. Others appreciate the opportunity, the résumé credit, and the paycheck. It's awfully nice when those **residuals** start dribbling in. You will decide what's right for you.

Most television spots are completed within a couple of days. The director, producers, crew, and clients (the "product" people) want actors who can take directions well, do a professional job, and go home. A television commercial set contains up to fifty people, all working under tremendous pressure, so it's essential that everything go as smoothly as possible.

# Voice-overs and Audio Drama

Tune in to your favorite radio station. This time, instead of concentrating on the music, listen to the ads. Those voices reading the ad copy belong to actors. Unlike

**Patrick** I did a Hoover vacuum cleaner TV commercial when I was little. And a cheese commercial. I've done radio commercials mostly—playing younger kids, like babies crying. When you play someone younger, you have to think small and make your voice a little bit higher. If you play someone older, you make your voice bigger and deeper.

**Joey** I did one commercial when I was four, a Nick, Jr. promo. Recently, someone I know saw it at Disney World. That was really funny.

**residuals:** the additional pay an actor receives for reruns or the repeated use of a film or a TV or radio commercial in which he or she appears

**David** *I like jingles best, personally, because you learn a catchy tune really quickly and you get your energy up.*

voice-overs for TV ads, which are designed to accompany a visual story, radio commercials rely completely on the actor's voice to carry the message.

Does anyone in your family have a book on tape? If not, check one out from your local library. You'll find a huge selection. As you listen, pay close attention to how each actor manages to communicate not only the story, but also the essence of character, using only his or her voice. Pretty amazing when you consider there are no images to go along with the words. In addition to books on tape, there are dramas on tape created specially for the voice. And the Internet is filled with audio dramas, Webcasts, and archives of classical radio spots from the days when there was no television. Can you imagine that people used to sit around the radio in the evening the same way we sit around the television?

How do you know if you're cut out for voice-overs or audio dramas? If you enjoy using your voice and are comfortable in front of a microphone, you're on your way. It never hurts, and may help a lot, to take a class in commercial work and/or voice-overs to get an idea of the kinds of qualities commercial directors look for. Think about the snappy, supercheerful voices you hear reciting ad copy, whether they're on television or the radio. The actor's job is to sell, sell, sell. No one wants to buy, buy, buy from someone who sounds glum or sluggish.

Of course, these same qualities will quickly become tiresome if you are playing a role that demands that your voice express a range of emotions and qualities. Here, as with all of your other acting work, your voice exercises and your listening skills will come in handy. Close your eyes and listen to the world. How does it sound? Complicated? Try to zoom in, with your ears, on a conversation. Okay, so you're eavesdropping. But this is research! Sort out which qualities in people's voices strike you as pleasing or irritating.

You'll find that in addition to becoming more aware of accents and the many rhythms of speech, you'll notice details about volume, tone, and pitch. You'll discover that you don't need your eyes to pick up on the emotions behind the words. Here's an experiment. Ask someone to say, "It's a beautiful day!" with a big smile. Then have him or her say it again with a scowl. You need to keep your eyes closed while he or she speaks. You can actually hear the difference. Why is the sound that comes out of a downturned mouth different from one stretched into a grin?

⭐ **Joey**  *Voice-overs, where they want just your voice, are the easiest. You go in, do it, and walk out. Sometimes they give you direction, but it's not that hard. The hardest auditions are when they hand you a script and you have to sing and act. I did a few voice-overs recently, one for Verizon Wireless and one for Thoroughbred horse racing.*

# Making Ends Meet

One of the many truths about acting is that at some point almost every actor has to earn his or her way while studying and pursuing a performing career. There are many ways to go about this, including part-time work at a bookstore or restaurant and finding jobs that are related to acting. Below are a few areas that offer actors a chance to use and improve their performance skills.

**Print Work**  There are lots of ads in magazines, catalogs, and newspapers that show kids doing everyday stuff like playing with a dog, eating, talking on the phone, or hanging out with friends or family. They might be selling dog food, a new after-school snack, a phone service, or a health or insurance plan. Some of the kids in these ads are professional clothing models who also do other kinds of ads, and some of them are

**David** *I love acting, I really do, but I don't think it's what I want to do my entire life. I've put some of my acting money into the stock market and check it every day. I think I'm going to study to be an investment banker, but I can't tell 100 percent. If I got to be a really famous actor, with limousines and bodyguards, I might reconsider.*

**Patrick** *I go to a professional performing arts school. Most of the kids there are actors, or are becoming actors. I have acting friends, but I have to put friends aside if I'm working. You can't get too involved.*

**Valeria** *Think about the thing that you would find craziest to do in real life and do it when you act. If it's not fun to act, don't do it.*

**Molly** *Try your hardest and do the best you can.*

actors whose looks and behavior fit into the message that advertisers want to project about their products. You'll notice that print ads, just like ads on television, tend to feature certain "types." Among others, there are well-groomed and studious, mischievous and scruffy, chubby and cheerful, athletic, and soulful. Do you see yourself fitting into any of them?

**Print work is more about role-playing than acting** in the traditional sense. There's obviously no speaking involved, and though you might have to learn a few simple movements if the idea is to catch you in action, most often the director will have you pose for the photographer in a particular position.

If you're interested in pursuing print work seriously, you'll need to find an agent who handles it. You'll need a résumé, of course, but instead of a simple headshot or two, you'll want to get a **composite** done, a photograph that combines several photos of you dressed and posed as several character types. And when you go to an interview for a print job, be sure to do some research ahead of time so that you can dress and act the part.

**Industrials** Another way that some actors earn money is through **industrials,** short films or videos that are made for businesses. An industrial might teach employees how to use a certain product or explain something about a company's history, philosophy, or work procedures. Industrials are similar to print work in that the people who make them also look for "types" whose looks and behavior can convey a particular message. Your composite and résumé will come in handy if you choose to give them a try.

**Extras** Every movie includes **extras,** actors who usually don't have lines but whose presence in the background of a scene gives it a sense of credibility. They might be walking down a street, eating in a restaurant, playing on a beach, or talking on the telephone. Being an extra can be a great introduction to film work, and occasionally some actors who are hired as background players get the opportunity to do more. If you keep your eyes and ears open, you can learn a lot in a day or two on a set. But if you want to move on to larger, speaking roles, it's important to be careful about not having casting agents think of you only as an extra.

# Actors' Unions

The decision to join one or more unions will depend where you are in your career as well as your goals and job requirements. It's important to know that unions work to make sure that member actors are paid fairly and on time for their work and aren't required to work an unreasonable number of hours. Some unions also offer meetings with casting agents and directors and acting and career workshops. Joining a union does not give you a better shot at an acting job. Only your professionalism and talent can do that. It does mean, however, that you cannot audition for nonunion jobs. Because of this, many actors choose to wait until they have several years of experience before joining, so their work options aren't limited. If you are interested, call for details regarding membership, services, and dues.

★ For Theater Work

**Actors Equity Association (AEA)**
**National Office**
**165 West 46th Street,**
**15th floor**
**New York, NY 10036**
**212-869-8530**
**www.actorsequity.org**

★ For Film, Television Shows, Commercials

**Screen Actors Guild (SAG)**
**National Headquarters**
**1515 Broadway, 44th floor**
**New York, NY 10036**
**212-944-1030**
**www.sag.com**

★ For Television and Radio

**American Federation of**
**Television and Radio Artists**
**(AFTRA)**
**260 Madison Avenue, 7th floor**
**New York, NY 10016**
**212-532-0800**
**www.aftra.com**

★ For Singers, Dancers, and Other Performers in Musicals, Operas, and Concerts

**American Guild of Musical**
**Artists, Inc. (AGMA)**
**National Office**
**1727 Broadway**
**New York, NY 10019**
**212-265-3687**
**www.musicalartists.org**

★ For Performers in Theme Parks, Variety Shows, Ice Shows, Nightclubs,* and Cabarets*

**(*These last two categories don't apply to you at this point in time.)**
**American Guild of Variety**
**Artists (AGVA)**
**National Headquarters**
**185 Fifth Avenue, 6th floor**
**New York, NY 10010**
**212-675-1003**
**www.agvany@aol.com**

# Appendixes

Read On! • Web Sites • Credits •
Monologues, Dialogues &
Ensemble Scenes

# Read On!

Here are some books that will give you further insights into and information about acting as well as the stuff that goes on behind the scenes.

### Acting

Allen, David. *Stanislavski for Beginners.*

Blumenfeld, Robert. *Accents: A Manual for Actors.*

Boal, Augusto. *Games for Actors and Non-actors.*

Brestoff, Richard. *The Great Acting Teachers and Their Methods.*

Chekhov, Michael. *To the Actor: On the Technique of Acting.*

Easty, Edward Dwight. *On Method Acting.*

Greenspan, Jaq. *Acting (V.G.M. Career Portraits).*

Gronbeck-Tedesco, John L. *Acting Through Exercises.*

Moore, Sonia. *The Stanislavski System.*

Rodenburg, Patsy. *The Actor Speaks: Voice and the Performer.*

Spolin, Viola. *Theater Games for the Classroom.*

### Monologues and Dialogues

Bert, Norman A., ed. *The Scene Book for Actors.*

Bland, Joellen, ed. *Playing Scenes from Classic Literature.*

Karczewski, Deborah. *Teens Have Feelings Too: 100 Monologues for Young Performers.*

Kehret, Peg. *Winning Monologues for Young Actors.*

Marlow, Jean. *Audition Speeches for Six- to Sixteen-Year-Olds.*

Milstein, Janet B. *The Ultimate Audition Book for Teens, Volume I: 111 One-Minute Monologues.*

Roddy, Ruth Mae. *More Monologues for Kids.*

Slaight, Craig, and Jack Sharrar. *Great Scenes and Monologues for Children, Volumes I and II.*

Tippet, Carole. *Red Licorice: Monologues for Young Actors.*

## Plays

Jennings, Coleman A., ed. *Theater for Young Audiences: Twenty Great Plays for Children.*

McCullogh, L. E., ed. *Plays of America from American Folklore for Young Actors Grades 7–12.*

Sklar, Daniel Judah. *Playmaking—Children Writing and Performing Their Own Plays.*

Slaight, Craig, ed. *New Plays from A.C.T.'s Young Conservatory.*

Timmerman, Diane. *90-Minute Theater* (*Romeo & Juliet* and *A Midsummer Night's Dream*).

## Auditioning and Making a Living

Ellis, Roger. *An Auditioning Handbook for Student Actors.*

Kanner, Ellie. *Next: An Actor's Guide to Auditioning.*

Mayfield, Katherine. *Acting A to Z: The Young Person's Guide to a Stage or Screen Career.*

Parke, Lawrence. *The Film Actor's Complete Career Guide.*

———. *How to Start Acting in Film and TV Wherever You Are in America.*

Rideout, Nigel. *First Steps Toward an Acting Career.*

## Behind the Scenes

Govier, Jacquie. *Create Your Own Stage Costumes.*

Lord, William A. *Stagecraft 1: A Complete Guide to Backstage Work.*

Thudium, Linda. *Stage Makeup.*

## The Movies

Halliwell, Leslie. *The Filmgoer's Companion.*

Sennett, Ted. *Lunatics and Lovers: A Tribute to the Giddy and Glittering Era of the Screen's "Screwball" and Romantic Comedies.*

# Web Sites

Here are theater Web sites you might want to check out. As you know, the Internet is a constantly changing landscape: sites come and go on a daily basis. So, if you find that a site listed here is no longer in existence (grrrr!), don't despair. There are lots of others, and within these are many, many links that will take you even further. Plus, you'll no doubt discover some on your own. Happy surfing!

**www.abwag.com.** Acting a Better Way with Actors Globally. This site offers all sorts of acting tips, bits of trivia, links, and simple lessons.

**www.actorsequity.org.** The site for Actors Equity, the actors' and stage managers' union.

**www.actorsite.com.** A Los Angeles–based site with lots of information about the business of acting.

**www.actorsource.com.** Information about getting started, auditioning, and agents.

**www.aftra.com.** The site for AFTRA, the American Federation of Television and Radio Artists union.

**www.backstage.com.** The on-line site for *Back Stage,* the performing arts weekly newspaper.

**www.bestwebs.com/vaudeville.** Information about real vaudeville shows, complete with sound clips.

**www.bigdreamers.com.** A site for young actors about the business, created by a young actor.

**www.clownantics.com.** Clown costumes, gear, and an on-line newsletter, *Funny Paper.*

**www.contemporarydrama.com.** Scripts for plays, monologues, musicals, radio, and TV shows; theater books and games; puppet and mime videos, sketches, books, and makeup.

**www.costumes.org.** Costume history, advice, designs, and links.

**www.dramatists.com.** Information about plays published by Dramatists Play Service, Inc., and lots of interesting links.

**www.footlightnotes.tripod.com.** An electronic magazine, *Footlight Notes,* about popular entertainment during a "period of extraordinary activity in the history of the theatre: the 1850s to the 1920s."

**www.free.prohosting.com/~jez.** Basic acting techniques and links.

**www.fun-shop.com/clown.htm.** Clown costumes, gear, and an on-line catalog.

**www.globalstage.net.** On-line video catalog of family theater from around the world.

**www.groundlings.com.** The site for the Groundlings improv troupe.

**www.hollywoodreporter.com.** An on-line magazine all about Hollywood.

**www.improvamerica.com.** Info about improv troupes and classes; lots of links.

**www.kidkomedy.com.** Some funny jokes by kids.

**www.musicals.net.** Song lists, story synopses, and links to info about many of the most famous musicals.

**www.nytheatre-wire.com.** Up-to-the-minute news about what's happening on New York City stages.

**www.playbill.com.** The on-line version of the in-theater program magazine *Playbill,* with reviews and information.

**www.redbirdstudio.com/AWOL/acting2.html.** Acting Workshop On Line (AWOL), a site with tons of info about the craft of acting, books, and links.

**www.sag.com.** The site for SAG, the Screen Actors Guild union.

**www.samuelfrench.com.** The site of the famous theatrical publisher, lots of plays and books about theater.

**www.schoolshows.demon.co.uk/index.htm.** A great resource for kids who are interested in getting involved in theater, plays to download, and acting tips.

**www.secondcity.com.** The site for the Second City improv troupe.

**www.shakespeare.com.** Loads of info about the Bard and all of his plays.

**www.singlelane.com/escript.** An on-line scriptwriting workshop.

**www.siue.edu/COSTUMES/actors/pics.html.** Photographs of English actors at the turn of the last century.

**www.spolin.com/players.html.** Site for the Spolin Players improv troupe.

**www.stagebill.com.** The site for the in-theater program magazine *Stagebill,* with reviews and information.

**www.theatre-link.com.** A guide to sites and information about theater on the World Wide Web, loads of links.

**www.us.imdb.com/search.** An Internet movie database.

**www.vl-theatre.com.** Great links to on-line theater resources and books.

**www.theatrecrafts.com/glossary.html.** An on-line glossary of technical theater terms.

# Credits

The following companies, organizations, and professionals helped make this book possible. A big thank-you to:

**Actors Studio**
432 W. 44th Street
New York, NY 10036
(212) 757-0870

**The American Academy of Dramatic Arts**
120 Madison Avenue
New York, NY 10016
(212) 686-9244

**Biz Kids**
125 Barrow Street, 4A
New York, NY 10014
(212) 243-6638

**Brooklyn Academy of Music**
30 Lafayette Avenue
Brooklyn, NY 11217
(718) 636-4177

**Calumet Photographic**
16 W. 19th Street
New York, NY 10011
(212) 989-8500

**City Lights Youth Theater**
300 W. 43rd Street, Suite 402
New York, NY 10036
(212) 262-0200

**Commonwealth Shakespeare Company**
P.O. Box 1023
Boston, MA 02177
(617) 423-7600

**Michal Daniel,**
photographer
3237 Longfellow Avenue
South Minneapolis,
MN 55407

**The Joseph Papp Theater/New York Shakespeare Festival**
425 Lafayette Street
New York, NY 10003
(212) 539-8500

**The Lee Strasberg Theatre Institute**
115 E. 15th Street
New York, NY 10003
(212) 533-5500

**Noelle Marinelli,**
makeup artist
nmarinelli@earthlink.net

**Karla Martinez,** stylist
(212) 683-3212

**Polaroid Corporation**
1265 Main Street W3
Waltham, MA 02451
(781) 386-3137

**Ricki G. Ravitts,**
stage combat coach
Society of American Fight
Directors (SAFD)
(800) 659-6579
mllemaupin@yahoo.com

**SoHo Studios**
13-17 Laight Street
New York, NY 10013
(212) 226-1100

**Studio with a View**
450 W. 31st Street
New York, NY 10001
(212) 629-3764

**TADA!**
120 West 28th Street
New York, NY 10001
(212) 627-1732

# Monologues, Dialogues & Ensemble Scenes

## Friendship by Lise Friedman (**Monologue**)

*This modern monologue expresses the complex feelings that go along with friendship.*

I have complicated relationships with my friends.

Sometimes my friendships seem really strong,

then the next minute they seem to completely vanish.

Who knows why that happens? It's frustrating.

And sometimes it's almost funny, like when someone says,

"I can't be your friend anymore because there's always so much drama with you."

I'm like, "Uh, okay," because she's the one making all the drama happen.

But she thinks she's really being tough and honest.

I think it's so stupid when someone pretends not to care about anything.

It's absurd—working so hard not to care.

You can't get much more ridiculous than that.

## Dreaming by Lise Friedman (**Monologue**)

*We've all had unusual dreams. The boy in this modern monologue describes a dream that left him feeling powerful.*

I had a crazy dream a few nights ago.

It was kind of like a movie.

There were all sorts of weird-looking creatures swimming around in the ocean.

Some looked a lot like whales, but they had arms and legs and could talk.

Others had long hair and faces like humans.

I was there, too, swimming way under water.

Even though I didn't have gills I could breathe.

Don't ask me why, but I followed a gigantic octopus into a cave that was filled with piles and piles of gold and jewels.

I tried to pick some up but it was all too slippery.

At the end of the dream, I flew out of the water into my room and felt really powerful.

That feeling stayed with me all day.

It was really cool.

## THE TEMPEST by William Shakespeare (**Monologue**)

*The magician Prospero counsels his son.*

Act IV. Scene 1. Before PROSPERO'S cell

**Prospero:** You do look, my son, in a moved sort,

As if you were dismay'd: be cheerful, sir.

Our revels now are ended. These our actors,

As I foretold you, were all spirits and

Are melted into air, into thin air:

And, like the baseless fabric of this vision,

The cloud-capp'd towers, the gorgeous palaces,

The solemn temples, the great globe itself,

Ye all which it inherit, shall dissolve

And, like this insubstantial pageant faded,

Leave not a rack behind. We are such stuff

As dreams are made on, and our little life

Is rounded with a sleep. Sir, I am vex'd;

Bear with my weakness; my brain is troubled:

Be not disturb'd with my infirmity:

If you be pleased, retire into my cell

And there repose: a turn or two I'll walk,

To still my beating mind.

## Pride and Prejudice by Jane Austen (**Monologue**)

*Elizabeth Bennet discovers that Mr. Darcy (whom she eventually marries) is really a good person, and is ashamed of her behavior toward him.*

How despicably have I acted!

I, who have prided myself on my discernment!

I, who have valued myself on my abilities!

Who have often disdained the generous candor of my sister, and gratified my vanity, in useless or blamable distrust.

How humiliating is this discovery!

Yet, how just a humiliation!

Had I been in love, I could not have been more wretchedly blind.

But vanity, not love, has been my folly.

Pleased with the preference of one, and offended by the neglect of the other,

on the very beginning of our acquaintance, I have courted prepossession and ignorance,

and driven reason away, where either were concerned.

Till this moment, I never knew myself.

## Alice in Wonderland by Lewis Carroll (**Dialogue**)

*Alice, who has just taken a bite of cake that shrinks her to three inches tall, peeks over the top of a mushroom to discover a pipe-smoking caterpillar.*

**Caterpillar:** Who are *you?*

**Alice:** I—I hardly know, sir, just at present—at least I know who I *was* when I got up this morning, but I think I must have been changed several times since then.

**Caterpillar:** What do you mean by that? Explain yourself!

**Alice:** I can't explain *myself,* I'm afraid, sir, because I'm not myself, you see.

**Caterpillar:** I don't see.

**Alice:** I'm afraid I can't put it more clearly, for I can't understand it myself to begin with; and being so many different sizes in a day is very confusing.

**Caterpillar:** It isn't.

**Alice:** Well, perhaps you haven't found it so yet, but when you have to turn into a chrysallis—you will some day, you know—and then after that into a butterfly, I should think you'll feel it a little queer, won't you?

**Caterpillar:** Not a bit.

**Alice:** Well, perhaps *your* feelings may be different; all I know is, it would feel very queer to *me.*

**Caterpillar:** You! Who are *you?*

**Alice:** I think you ought to tell me who *you* are, first.

MACBETH by William Shakespeare (**Ensemble**)

*Three witches are brewing a spell in this tale of murder.*

Act 1. Scene 1. A desert place.

*[Thunder and lightning. Enter three Witches.]*

**First Witch:** When shall we three meet again

In thunder, lightning, or in rain?

**Second Witch:** When the hurlyburly's done,

When the battle's lost and won.

**Third Witch:** That will be ere the set of sun.

**First Witch:** Where the place?

**Second Witch:** Upon the heath.

**Third Witch:** There to meet with Macbeth.

**First Witch:** I come, Graymalkin!

**Second Witch:** Paddock calls.

**Third Witch:** Anon.

**ALL:** Fair is foul, and foul is fair:

Hover through the fog and filthy air.

*[Exeunt]*

# Photo Credits

All photographs are by Mary Dowdle unless noted below.

**Blue Man Group,** page 96

**Venustiano Borromeo,** pages 142, 143 *(top, middle, and bottom),* 144, 145, 146, 147, 159 *(left and right),* 160, 161, 162 *(top and bottom),* 163 *(top and bottom)*

**Matthew M. Cazier,** page 35

**Michael Creason and Mark Bennett,** pages 152, 153

**Michal Daniel,** pages 16, 59 *(top),* 63, 76, 79, 91, 92, 97, 98, 129 *(top and bottom)*

**The Everett Collection,** page 61

**The Lester Glassner Collection,** pages 65, 182

**Bret Gustafson/Johnson County Community College,** page 156 *(top)*

**Joan Marcus,** page 156 *(bottom)*

**N.Y. Public Library Picture Collection,** pages xii, 7, 134, 170 *(top and bottom)*

**Laurie Olinder/Ridge Theater,** pages x, xi

**Benjamin Pearcy,** page 149

**Photofest,** pages v, 20, 21, 23, 24, 27, 33 *(right),* 42, 47, 48, 57, 58, 59 *(bottom),* 60 *(top, middle, and bottom),* 67, 68, 71, 74 *(top and bottom),* 78, 81, 95, 107, 110, 113, 118, 132, 164, 168 *(left and right),* 169 *(top left and right, and bottom),* 173, 174, 175, 176, 178, 180 *(left and right),* 181

**Playbill image courtesy of Playbill, Inc.,** page 66